GET THE

SKINNY

SILVER
INVESTING

DAVID MORGAN

GET THE SKINNY™ BOOKS

An Imprint of Morgan James Publishing

Garden City, New York • www.morganjamespublishing.com

GET THE SKINNY ON: SILVER INVESTING

ISBN: 1-933596-79-1 (Paperback)
ISBN: 1-60037-056-X (Hardcover)
ISBN: 1-60037-057-8 (eBook)
ISBN: 1-60037-058-6 (Audio)

Published by:

www.morganjamespublishing.com

Morgan James Publishing, LLC
1225 Franklin Ave Ste 325
Garden City, NY 11530-1693
Toll Free 800-485-4943
www.MorganJamesPublishing.com

Cover & Interior Design by:
3 Dog Design
www.3dogdesign.net
chris@3dogdesign.net

Acknowledgements

Many people have helped me over the years and been very supportive of my work. The following list of acknowledgements is far from complete so any of my close associates that have participated in aiding my work please know though it may not be publicly recognized here, I am grateful to all of you. This especially applies to my subscribers both good and bad that have provided input over the years some affirming some most critical, but it has been the goal from the beginning to do our best and use the feedback to improve.

First, I would like to thank The Silver Institute for being open minded enough to let me present my papers at some of the forums even though viewed as controversial by many in the financial mainstream. It is a tribute to the Free Market of Ideas that all views can be presented.

I would like to acknowledge Mr. Franklin Sanders of the Money Changer who has provided me with help whenever asked and provided great insights into the history of silver. I am grateful to Mr. Charles Savoie who has written the best researched and documented case on silver and the banking establishment going back into history. The website www.silver-investor.com is the only site in the world that has the complete Savoie collection.

Mr. Ted Butler has been a large influence on my work and we have spoken many times on the silver market, leasing, commitment of trader's reports and most aspects of the silver market. We have included an entire chapter by Mr. Butler because no one speaks more succulently about that subject than Mr. Butler.

Mr. James Puplava must be acknowledged as one of the first to give me a chance to explain the dynamics of the silver market to his very broad audience. In fact Jim has become a very well studied precious metals advocate himself and helped countless thousands of investors worldwide.

Mr. Sean Rakhimov has been instrumental in helping my work in many ways and has become a regular contributor to our monthly research report. Sean approached me several years ago and asked to work with me, at first this was impossible but as our website became more popular we have formed a close association.

Mr. Bill Murphy of The Gold Anti-Trust Action committee and all the GATA faithful must be acknowledged although their focus is primarily on gold they do admit to being most favorable to silver as well. I attended Gold Rush 21 in the Yukon Territories in 2005 and met Mr. Hugo Salinas Price in person for the first time. Mr. Price well understands money and the consequences of the current state of affairs in the world's monetary system, and is the leading proponent of enacting silver as money in Mexico.

Mr. James Turk of www.goldmoney.com recently added silver to this impressive precious metals based Internet system. James is a visionary in my view and sees the future of money from a perspective few envision at this point in time.

I would like to acknowledge Mr. Joe Martin of Cambridge House and Mr. Pat Gorman of Resource Consultants both of these gentlemen provided me with a public forum to teach the basic bullish case for the silver market to both individual and institutional investors alike.

Acknowledgments

One of my associates Mr. David Bond lives in the famous Silver Valley and has been valuable in getting the inside track in many venues in the silver market.

Finally, I must acknowledge my strong faith in God, the source that makes all things possible. Today expressing one's faith is not popular yet many have faith in paper currency not knowing what this book should help them understand. The basic principles of freedom still apply as long as men and women are willing to stand for those principles.

On that note, I challenge the reader to look beyond this book and gather information to satisfy yourself as to the true nature of money, precious metals, the financial system and your position as being one of the knowledgeable or not.

GET THE **SKINNY** ON:

Contents

Introduction

The main purpose in writing this book was to make the investment community at large aware of what I believe to be the single best investment in the world at the present time-silver!

Everyone that has ever thought of making money in the market should read this book and understand that opportunities like this are rare in the world of money and it takes courage to buy when very few are even aware of the potential.

The Supply and Demand fundamentals are so overwhelming that anyone who understands basic economics will become excited about how significant this is for the silver market.

We will examine some of the myths about silver and one that almost all have heard is that digital photography is going to kill the silver market. This little understood aspect of the market will be examined and the findings will surprise most people.

Any market has to balance supply and demand, and the silver market is no exception but how silver demand has been satisfied could be a subject of another book, we look briefly into precious metals leasing and its impact on price.

Silver like gold is considered to be a commodity foremost by the market. Therefore regardless of their role as money throughout history we must examine how silver is traded on the commodity exchanges.

Silver has been considered to be money and in fact is the first money mentioned in the Bible. The word for silver and the word for money are synonymous in most Latin based languages. Although this is understood in Mexico, South America and Asia, most North Americans and Europeans don't have a clue.

Of all the metals required for life, as we know it, silver is the one standout; more uses for silver are discovered each year than all other metals combined. New uses affect demand, and demand will affect price, we examine some of the new uses for silver in the future.

Silver is price inelastic in most of its applications. This simply means that the little bit of silver required to make a refrigerator has very little effect on the overall price of that refrigerator. This is a very important point because if silver were to jump up dramatically in price the refrigerator manufacturer would still have to purchase silver and it would not effect the price of the refrigerator that much, since so little silver is used per unit.

There are many ways to invest in the silver market and we will examine bullion, coins, mining stocks and leveraged investments such as futures and options.

Finally, we look at possible price scenarios and this should really get the reader excited.

This book can be used as a brief education of the qualities and investment possibilities of an element so vital to the technological age we live in that its very existence is essential to daily life. By the time the reader has finished this book they should have a good idea on where to go to get more information to apply what they have learned.

Introduction

This book is valuable because the vast majority of investors know nothing about the precious metals markets and because these markets are so small any new investment demand will drive these markets significantly higher.

There has not been a book written specifically about the silver market since the early 1990's and most people familiar with precious metals are the baby boomers or older. There is a whole generation or two that need to be educated about this market.

Although much effort and research went into this book, it really is merely a summary of the highpoints of silver and silver investing. The reader is encouraged to do their own verification and explore the subject, our website www.silver-investor.com is dedicated to the serious precious metals investor, and we have one of the best collections of information about silver anywhere in the world.

Lastly, we know how much competition there is for the investment dollar and almost everyone is interested in making money. This subject fascinated us for a lifetime and yet it is so interesting how few understand truly what money is, and without that knowledge you chances of "making it" are greatly reduced.

Foreword

The first step in any endeavor is most likely the hardest. I have been thinking, planning, and talking about writing this book for far too long. Many of my loyal subscribers and many casual web surfers that have read part or all of my website have asked when are you going to finish your book on silver?

Part of my problem is I wanted to cover silver in a manner that I would find to be the most fascinating and compelling case for silver based investments ever written. Secondly, like most humans overcoming procrastination takes action. Most would not call me lazy; in fact the work in my newsletter and my personal fitness goals of running my first mini-triathlon at age 50 speaks to my work ethic.

So after enough thought I decided to take action and begin. My interest in silver began quite by accident and at a very early age. My interest in the metal began at age eleven. I came from a typical middle class background born in the early 1950's. My Dad worked my mother did not and we had a good life. My parents were going to raise me to respect "the value of a dollar" and I truly think they succeeded perhaps beyond what they ever imagined.

You see when I was ten years old my family decided that I could earn an allowance, this 25 cent piece was a 90% Silver coin in 1964 and I could earn one each week by cleaning my room and watering the fruit orchard my father had planted. A funny thing happened the next year; I did not get a wage increase from the going inflation rate, however, the coinage changed. The 1965 quarters were devoid of all silver and were "silver looking" but were a sandwich of copper and zinc. I knew without any formal economic training the two quarters could not possibly be equal in value although I heard President Johnson state that they were.

This was my first lesson that bad money drives out good—Gresham's law and that even Presidents can misinform the public. I carried this observation about money with me from that point forward and developed a burning desire to understand money itself.

I put my money study pretty much on hold but as I grew older my studies included the great inflations of the past. What I discovered fascinated me because it seemed that history was repeating itself, the United States was traveling down the same road as ancient Rome, the currency was being debased and there was little that could be done about it. In fact even at an early age and the beginning of my quest it looked as if gold might be the solution but at that time it was illegal for Americans to own gold, although gold could be purchased elsewhere in the world.

By the time I was graduating from high school Richard M. Nixon pulled the plug on gold and stated to the world that the United States was no longer converting the dollar into gold. This was a grave concern to me personally, but it seemed little concern to anyone else, was I the only one that took my parents lesson seriously – the value of a dollar? The value was now arbitrary and had no meaning. Certainly there were brave men and women that stood up and shouted to the deaf masses that this would lead to grave problems in the future. Jim Blanchard being one such individual that actually traveled to Washington D.C. and protested this move to a fiat currency.

No longer would the catch phrases "Sound as a Dollar" or "Good as Gold" ring true, yet people still used these expressions the masses seemed to either not understand or not care, the paper promises were not valid for silver after 1968 and gold was something that very few had ever seen or cared about. After all these pieces of paper were working just fine and everyone accepted them, so what was the concern anyway?

By the time I was ready for college I had another question that simply would not cease, if the Constitution was the supreme authority to protect our inalienable rights, and it specified that gold and silver were to be coined how did the Federal Reserve get into power and was their authority legitimate? This question still is debated among academics today.

Chapter ①

Supply and Demand

Most investors are looking for information that will reveal an opportunity that will insure success and guarantee to help them "make money" in the financial markets. Few if any ever question what constitutes money, and in fact the very act of saving in real money may be one of the biggest opportunities for investors over the next several years.

Very few investors are interested in silver, as an investment, and many that have tried in the past have gotten bored or burned and will not enter the market again. Although the basic premise of "Buy low, Sell high" certainly applies here, it is a good study of human nature on how few actually apply this basic principle. When our work first appeared on the Internet nearly six months went by before we received even one inquiry. At that time silver was at an all time low adjusted for inflation. Although a screaming buy hardly anyone was paying attention. Silver on an inflation adjusted basis is still at a very low price, and in our view the precious metals markets are in the second phase or leg-up where the gains will still be very favorable.

Most investors don't pay attention to silver; if someone discusses precious metals most people turn their attention to gold. However, unlike gold or oil, there are no "Big Players" like central banks or OPEC in the silver market. This is important because there is no big overhang of supply that can enter the market and suppress the price. There may be a possible exception here because Warren Buffett, arguably one of the world's best investors did purchase 129.7 million ounces of silver bullion in 1997.

One of the most incredible truths about silver is that demand has outstripped supply for sixteen straight years, starting 1990 to present. This trend is projected to continue for at least the next several years. Annual silver supply deficits have run as high as 200 million ounces in boom years, and as low as 40 million ounces in other years. It is important to realize that even in years of decreased silver demand, the mining supply on an annual basis did NOT meet demand. There is nothing more bullish for a commodity than such a deficit condition.

It should be pointed out that a deficit is not a shortage. Supply must always equal demand. A deficit simply means that the amount of silver mined annually does not meet the annual demand. The difference between what is mined and what is used is made up by above ground supply.

The silver stockpiles (above ground supply in storage) increased after the huge run-up in silver prices during the last cycle from 1971 to 1980. From 1979 to 1989 silver inventories increased by approximately one billion ounces in addition to what was already held in above ground inventories. This figure and almost all figures dealing with silver inventory supply are unofficial. At best these are educated guessed but guesses nonetheless. This above ground silver supply has been drawn down since 1990 and some of the best silver studies in the world have estimated that perhaps 1.5 Billion ounces of silver have been used up from 1990 to 2005.

As of early 2006 the estimated amount of available silver bullion varies depending upon which study you choose to quote. However, both the CPM Group and Gold Field Mineral Services agree that the total above ground silver supply is approximately 500 million ounces, at this time (April 2006). One should put this number into context. First, realize that silver hit an all time high of $50.00 U.S. per ounce in 1980 when the amount of silver bullion was two billion ounces.

Secondly, consider again the fact that one of the world's best investors Mr. Warren Buffett announced a purchase of 129.7 million ounces of silver bullion in 1997. Mr. Buffett recently announced that he has sold his silver but we look at this as a bullish sign because the market was able to absorb all that silver and the price of silver has remained strong!

Another fact about the silver bullion supply is that the New York Mercantile Exchange reports silver inventories of about 125 million ounces in early 2006. This is the largest known visible supply of silver in the world. This number needs to be discussed because the NYMEX supply is broken down into two categories.

The registered category is what silver dealers generally hold, this silver can be bought and sold almost instantly. The second category is named eligible and investors largely hold this silver that use the various NYMEX approved facilities to store their silver. The eligible category requires an additional amount of paper work to be completed before this category of silver can be sold. So in practical terms the eligible category is silver held by investors.

This fact is important because it gives an indication of how much silver is being held by investors that expect higher prices. In early 2006 54 million ounces of silver were held in the eligible category.

Investors in silver bullion can own it through other investment vehicles. For example both the Central Fund of Canada and Bullion Management Services also of Canada hold physical metal for their investors. Between these two investments perhaps 30 million ounces of silver is being stored at the time of this writing.

Most people want proof that so much silver has disappeared. First consider what Reuters wire service stated in November 2000.

The U.S. National Defense silver stockpile is now exhausted. The U.S. National Defense Stockpile Center (NDSC) has committed to deliver its remaining stockpile of silver, nearly 15 million ounces, to the United States Mint for its coinage programs, the final balance of silver will be shipped to the mint over the next few weeks, effectively depleting the U.S. silver stockpile.

This is a profound fact that the U.S. government held 375 million ounces of silver in 1970 and it is now completely out of silver! In fact the U.S. mint must purchase silver in the open market in order to keep the silver coin programs continuing.

Remember the price of silver until recently had been at historic lows, and demand for silver was fed by above ground supply and government inventory comprised part of that supply. The U.S. Treasury held over two billion ounces of silver in 1959. But today the U.S. government has no silver, nada, NONE!

The government of India does have some silver and China also has some government secured silver. China actually met their needs for silver consumption up until 2004 at which point China mining activity fell short of current demand.

According to the most recently published Silver Survey 2005 from CPM Group available silver bullion supply is approximately 500 million ounces.

So, in review we see that there is a possibility that the amount of available silver may be in the range of 300 million ounces when considering that Silver ETF, NYMEX investors, and Investment Funds may own 200 million ounces of silver bullion.

The amount of silver bullion at the current time is a fact that is extremely bullish, but generally unknown. There is actually less silver bullion available for investment than gold! This one fact alone should alert any intelligent investor into thinking that some silver must be held as part of one's precious metals allocation.

At this point in time the amount of gold bullion is about 2 billion ounces in bullion form, and as discussed the amount of silver bullion is approximately 500 million ounces or one-fourth the amount of gold.

Before moving on, it is important to qualify this fact. First, this comparison is between gold bullion and silver bullion. In both cases, we are not talking about jewelry or art forms of the metals. However, to clarify the point, if silver coinage was added to the silver bullion, the total would still be approximately one billion ounces. To be consistent we would also have to add the coin back into the total, which would put gold at about 3 billion ounces. Thus, silver would still be less than one-third of the gold supply, if we count both gold coin and gold bullion.

The reason most of this discussion is on silver bullion is because the price for silver (and for gold) is set in the Futures Market for point .999 fine bullion. This means this subset (bullion) silver is the most critical not only for price-setting purposes but also for industry. Certainly, silver coinage does matter and the amount, although small, will play a role it determining the price of silver in the years ahead.

Many people demand proof that the silver situation is as bullish as is being presented. Many investors perhaps overlook this exercise. Gold is still held by many governments . . . silver is held by virtually none. China and India do have some silver inventory, but it is considered to be minimal, at best. Again, one easily verifiable fact is that the United States government is now totally out of silver at this point in time and now must go to the open market to purchase silver to continue its Silver American Eagle coin program. Think about this for a moment: The U.S. once held 2 billion ounces of silver . . . and now has none!

By far, silver is the more undervalued of the two precious metals. Gold has appreciated and broken out from its base in 2001. Meanwhile, silver generally remained in a narrow trading range of $4 to $5 dollars for more than a decade. Once silver finally did move above the $5.50 area, this unique metal began to exhibit strength. The silver market has already outperformed gold on a net basis, meaning that from the silver bottom in 1993 to the high of 2006, silver climbed from $3.50 per ounce to almost $13.00. Gold bottomed in 2001 around $252 and traded as high as $700 in 2006 so far.

The silver market is not only much smaller than the gold market physically, but it is also true monetarily. The total amount of silver, in price terms, might equal ten billion dollars (factoring in bullion and coins). Whereas gold bullion and coins would be worth over a trillion dollars, this fact displays itself in the price action of the two metals. Silver is far more volatile than gold and, thus, investors should bear this in mind. However, as precious metal markets continue to gather strength throughout this decade, just a small increase in new silver purchases could have a far greater impact on silver prices than the same amount of money invested in gold.

In studying the silver market for nearly my entire life, I have reached the conclusion there will not be a sustained or substantial increase in the price of silver until the physical supply is so small that the commercial users sense a coming shortage. At that point, silver will show price strength that few believe possible at this point. Why? Because, at that point, silver users in the defense, automobile and electronics industries will all be competing for silver at the same time that investors will sense the profit potential. It is with this understanding that I build my case that silver offers one of the single best long-term opportunities today.

Chapter ②

Silver a Rare Investment Opportunity
Silver supply a result of base metal mining

Where does the silver supply come from? Most silver is mined as a result of mining other minerals. In fact, nearly seventy five percent of silver coming to surface is the result of copper, lead, zinc and gold mining. This is an important fact because this does present some unique conditions for the silver market.

First, any mining activity that does not depend upon the price of silver for their profit really is not that interested in the merits of silver. This accounts for three-quarters of the industry. This is a rather unfortunate fact for silver investors but it can work in your favor, as we will explain later.

Most base metals miners simply view silver as a bonus of their mining activity. For example a copper miner certainly is not going to throw the silver out, but they simply want to not take any risk with the price fluctuations of silver and use the banking industry to sell any silver recovered with their primary product, copper in this example. This exerts price pressure on silver because this constant selling pressure exists from almost all the base metals producers and several of them sell forward more silver than they actually have above ground.

The primary silver producers are really the only miners that are primarily concerned with the price of silver and this comprises only twenty-five percent of the market. A primary silver miner is defined as a company whose primary profit and loss statement is dependent upon the cash flow received by the silver sold into the marketplace.

Most primary silver producers do not hedge their silver production whereas almost all byproduct miners do. The world is in a commodity boom currently due to the rapidly expanding industrial revolution in China. Secondly, mining activity has been depressed for almost two decades due to low commodity prices. The bottom was hit in early 2000 when the NASDAQ stock market in the U.S. was hitting all time highs. At that time the commodity cycle was ready to begin a multi-year bull market.

Mining activity in general has begun a new boom cycle and exploration for mineral wealth and energy resources have garnered support from people around the world. However, it can take several years to bring a new mine into production.

Base metal mining has been increasing the past few years and as a result more silver has been mined as well. For the year ending 2005 it was estimated that an additional 29 million ounces of silver were mined over the previous year due to increased base metal production.

Summary
In summary the supply of silver has been dwindling for the past several years and the above ground stocks are being drawn down. This fundamental factor in silver's favor will continue to exert upward price pressure until the market can be brought into equilibrium either through price, increased silver supply, or both.

Chapter 2: A Rare Investment Opportunity

The demand for silver is quite an interesting study. Silver has a unique demand structure far different from its big brother gold. Gold is primarily thought of as a money metal and most investment is because of this perception.

Silver is used in many applications and is vital to the technological age but has a very poor investment profile. Only eight percent or so of silver demand is for investment purposes, the rest is split into a few main categories.

The main categories are industrial fabrication, photography, jewelry and silverware. According to the Silver Institute industrial fabrication uses about forty-two percent of demand. Photography uses over twenty percent, and the silverware/jewelry category uses nearly thirty percent. The remaining silver demand is for coin and investment.

An unknown fact to most people is how much silver they consume each year without ever giving it any attention. For example silver is an essential element in computers, cell phones, microwave ovens, electrical contacts, solar energy cells, and a host of other applications.

Since demand for these items is expected to grow substantially, it is reasonable to project that demand for silver from these traditional applications will remain strong as well.

Chapter 3

The Photography Myth

Wall Street analysts often make the argument that the demand for silver will disappear, due to the advent, popularity and growth in the digital camera market. The Silver Institute completed a study on digital photography, which showed that there would be an impact, but that it is very slight indeed.

In February 2004, The Silver Institute made this bold statement: "Despite the emotional reaction to the sales decline of film in photography, we do not foresee any major shift in the need for silver in producing silver halide products over the next five years."

Many facts are ignored when the photography argument is presented. The color photography market uses no silver, because all silver on the film is brought back out into solution when the color print is made, and all this silver is recycled. The amount of silver recycled through photographic processing is truly worth noting.

If we examine how the silver supply is calculated each year we discover that twenty two percent of the silver supply is brought to the market each year as scrap. "Scrap" is the code word for silver from photo recycling. Certainly, there is very little in the way of people sending in their used silver items to be smelted down. Yes, some of this does take place, but it is insignificant relative to the amount of silver that comes from recycling of photographic materials. Almost the entire "scrap" market comes from film recycling.

Now some photographic silver does in fact remain in the end product. X-rays for example do hold silver and so in a practical sense this is silver that does not come back in the form of recycling. However, some X-rays do come back under present conditions due to the MRI replacing the X-ray machine in many cases and the digitizing of X-ray images.

Black and white photography also retains some of the silver similar to the X-ray example. But black and white photography is a very small segment of the overall photographic market.

Another point seldom discussed is how most people use their digital cameras. If email is used to send or receive photos, then a computer is required, and the computer uses silver. Additionally, if one decides to store the images on a CD, the CD is a piece of plastic with a very thin coating of silver so the laser can read the information.

Think about this for a moment, silver halide processing of color film returns the silver but how much silver is presently being recovered from CD's? To our knowledge very little if any and the CD industry seems to be in a growth cycle although with the rapidly changing technologies we cannot be certain that a few years hence, the CD won't be replaced with another cheaper and faster storage medium.

Certainly, it must be admitted that the digital film world will cut into the use of silver, but it would also mean less silver would be available to the market each year in the form of recycling. In fact if you took this thesis to the limit and presented the bearish case, no silver would be used in photography and this would imply practically no silver would be available by way of photographic processing.

This of course is not going to happen, silver halide processing will not go away entirely we merely wish to present the case that the photographic silver supply is a unique case and must be understood correctly.

Kodak and Fuji have invested heavily in China for silver halide processing plants. This large capital expenditure would not take place if the end of silver halide processing were imminent.
So does digital photography impact the silver market? Yes, in the areas of graphic arts and radiography, it does impact the market. The Silver Institute estimates that over the next three years, considering all types of photographic demand, silver use will decline by approximately three million ounces.

Another point I wish to make is the presupposition on the question. This question presumes that the only thing silver is used for is photography. No film use, hence, no need for silver. This is ridiculous.

The amount of silver lost to the digital world will not kill the silver market. There are more patents issued for silver on an annual basis than for all other metals combined. In other words, more uses are discovered all the time for silver. Silver is one of the best "technology stocks" you can buy, because silver is used not only in photography, but also in many high-tech applications that continually have outstanding demand.

The following article may give the reader some additional information about the digital photographic market. The interview can be found on the following website www.financialsense.com

The Big Picture on Silver!
By Eric King - July 28, 2003

A while ago I mentioned to my good friend David Morgan author of the website www.silver-investor.com that every time silver gets anywhere near $5.00, Kodak immediately issues a press release, something to the effect that digital photography is killing conventional photography.

Silver turns around usually intra-day and by the close ends down around 10 cents or over 2% on the trading session. Something very interesting happened last Wednesday morning in silver's latest attempt at the $5.00 area. Kodak had it's usual end of the world for conventional photography press release announcing it was laying off 6,000 workers because again digital photography was killing conventional photography. However, Kodak crushed analyst estimates of 29 cents/share more than doubling the estimates by earning 60 cents/share! "We are pleased to report quarterly earnings that are stronger than we had previously expected," said Kodak Chairman and Chief Executive Officer Daniel A. Carp.

Not bad for a company whose wheels are coming off because it's core business of photography is being destroyed (smile). Kodak CEO added, "Our traditional consumer film and processing operations continue to face challenges associated with the increasing popularity of digital photography...Consumer adoption of digital photography is growing at a more rapid pace than a year ago, and this is trimming demand for consumer film. At the same time, we are seeing evidence that more consumers want to print their digital photos at retail and at home."

Getting back to last Wednesday morning with silver approaching $5.00 once again, Kodak comes out with the usual "bad news" for conventional photography press release, but this time as I said something interesting happened in the silver market.

From Midas, "The silver move was nothing less than sensational...Among the biggest moves in many years." After silver exploded over 6% on Wednesday, silver closes out the week above $5.00 for the 3rd consecutive trading day and all of this on "bad news."

Very interesting in my opinion, you know what they say about something that has been in a long bear market in silver's case 23 years, that stops going down on bad news (even goes up). This came as no surprise to David Morgan (as a student of silver for over 20 years) because he has been on record for many years as saying that the silver bull market would begin in the summer of 2003.

Throughout my career as a value investor, I have consistently looked for under-valued assets and sectors to increase my net worth. Most recently a couple of examples are the oil sector in late 1999, early 2000, small cap restaurant stocks in 2001, but in late 2002 silver caught my attention. I believe silver is ending a 23-year bear market and is just about to begin a very significant bull market.

Since I have taken possession of over 3 tons of physical silver (so far) I decided to research the digital/conventional photography market. This search led me to a company, which recycles silver and has the greatest percentage of recovery of anyone in the world! No small feat of achievement in my opinion, the name of the company is Itronics. The Chairman and CEO of Itronics is Dr. John W. Whitney, one of the top minds in the world on silver recycling. Dr. Whitney kindly agreed to go on record and clear up some of the misinformation about digital photography and it's effects on the silver market. The following dialogue took place in the third week of July 2003:

King: "Thank you for spending time with me on the subject of digital photography Dr. Whitney. Maybe you can help myself us to gain a better understanding of digital photography and it's impact on the silver market. To start off, what percentage of silver used in color photography is recycled?"

Dr. Whitney: "80 to 85% of silver used in color photography is recycled. Silver used in color film is completely removed from the paper and all of the silver goes into the liquid so there is an incredible recovery rate."

King: "What about the recovery rate on X-Rays and black and white photography?"

Dr. Whitney: "When you say black and white what you really mean is black and clear. Only about 50% of silver is removed from the negatives into the liquid so recovery is much less than conventional photography."

King: "With regards to digital photography, I have heard there are problems with photographs having tremendous deterioration and fading over time when the photographs are not printed out on silver coated paper is that true?"

Dr. Whitney: "That is one of the 'dirty little secrets' of digital photography. Printed images fade and some papers being manufactured and sold have longer life, however none of it is permanent. Conventional prints are permanent and black and white is good for 100 years."

King: "So in the end consumers who want to keep these pictures permanently as stores of memories will have to use conventional methods of development in order to ensure they will last?"

Dr. Whitney: "I am servicing one of the big companies which takes in digital photography and they are using conventional methods for developing the pictures for that very reason."

King: "Conventional methods for developing the digital pictures, interesting. What about the picture quality of digital?"

Dr. Whitney: "High quality digital photography has 4,000 to 10,000 pixels. To contrast, conventional photography has 16,000,000 to 20,000,000 pixels so resolution is much sharper. There is a technological problem and it has existed as a problem since the early 50's, how to get those inks to stabilize so they don't fade on you. The word is getting out; I think even Kodak has admitted there is a problem. The other issue which is none of my business, but which bothers me a great deal is CD Rom is the new method of storage and it is not entirely stable. So when people store those photos they may not know they have to replace the CD's every 5 years or so because of deterioration."

King: "Isn't this going to be a major 'black eye' going forward for the digital world?"

Dr. Whitney: "As I said, storage is a problem and I would suspect that when people store those pictures they may not know they have to replace those (CD's) every 5 years or so because of deterioration. Consumers may react with anger and a sense of helplessness when they find out their photos they planned to save for a lifetime and pass on to their children have been lost because of a technical issue."

King: "Is silver being used in any other form in the digital world?"

Dr. Whitney: "Silver is now being used to coat the new CD ROMs, they have a silver mirror finish. I believe Kodak developed the technology and I believe it allowed them to bring the cost of the CD Rom down as well as they were previously using gold to coat the CD Rom."

King: "I am sure digital businesses are aware and working on these problems. What are your thoughts on attempts to remedy these problems?"

Dr. Whitney: "Technology is being improved, but right now it is a minimum of 10 years to even think they can successfully remedy some of these problems. For governments this is already an issue. Microfiche is a permanent successful method of storing images; of course again this involves silver usage. This is second hand, so this is in the gossip category, but from what I understand NASA put some of it's photos and text into new technology at one point, destroying the original microfiche and the technology failed causing the loss of a portion of a decade worth of photos and data to be lost forever. Recently, Hong Kong and Singapore have switched back to microfiche because of these types of problems; the only reliable way to store long-term is microfiche. This is a trend change back to conventional."

King: "So governments and government agencies have tragically lost records forever because of technology failures?"

Dr. Whitney: "That is my understanding."

King: "What are your thoughts on the silver market?"

Dr. Whitney: "Fundamentals and price don't correspond."

King: "So you think silver is headed higher?"

Dr. Whitney: "Where you have a problem is if individuals decided to buy silver as a 'store of value' then there would not be enough silver to supply the demand and there would be major dislocations in the silver market."

King: "Any other thoughts on the silver market?"

Dr. Whitney: "I'm one of the major shareholders in Itronics, so I am heavily invested in silver with my own portfolio and also with 16 years of work in recycling and helping to develop better and more efficient technology for the recovery process."

King: "What are your final thoughts on Digital's effect on conventional photography?"

Dr. Whitney: "Well, digital imaging and digital photography have decreased the growth rate."

King: "So the conventional photography market continues to grow?"

Dr. Whitney: "I believe that to be the case. Worldwide it continues to grow, most folks can't afford computers and even if they can it is still very complicated. By the way, a high growth area for conventional photography is disposable cameras."

King: "In the end as consumers lose some of their photos they had planned to keep for the rest of their lives, how do you think this is going to affect the digital world?"

Dr. Whitney: "I don't know the answer, but I know if my wife lost all of her photographs she would be extremely upset."

King: "One more question before I let you go. I am wondering, because you and your spouse are very knowledgeable about both conventional and digital, how do you choose to develop your photographs?"

Dr. Whitney: "My wife develops using the conventional method, because it permanently saves the pictures."

King: "Thank you Dr. Whitney for taking time to dispel some of the misinformation out there about digital photography and its effect on the silver market."

Dr. Whitney: "You're welcome."

Chapter 4

Silver Leasing

This entire chapter is curtosey of Investment Rarities from an article from Mr. Ted Butler. We left the disclosure statement intact as it is also my view that Ted is controversial yes, but has been the leader in unraveling what has really been taking place in the silver market for so many years. No matter what was written about silver leasing it would require that I acknowledge Ted Butler and upon careful contemplation, it just seemed best to read the man himself rather than any editorialized comment from this author.

SILVER LEASING OR SILVER FLEECING?

By Ted Butler - March 13, 2001

From James Cook, President of Investment Rarities:
"The following essay by Theodore Butler makes claims and arguments that are controversial. Although we have found Mr. Butler to be an accurate analyst of the silver market, we must nevertheless issue a disclaimer about the nature of his comments. These views did not originate with Investment Rarities and though we may agree, we lack the knowledge and insight to make such claims. This is Mr.. Butler's show and we are conveying it to you without necessarily endorsing these statements. Mr. Butler makes claims which at first blush appear to be somewhat libelous. He is aware of this but is not overly concerned about possible legal repercussions. We are presenting his statements, but we do not guarantee the accuracy or correctness of these somewhat inflammatory comments."

Leasing 101

Recently, it occurred to me that the most important aspect of the gold and silver market, is not understood widely. I am referring to gold and silver leasing. I'll attempt to define and analyze metal leasing here, but I must warn you - I'm not about to pull any punches. For almost five years, I have raised the issue that the leasing and forward selling of gold and silver is fraudulent and manipulative, and has artificially depressed the price of each. We are talking about some very large and well-known financial institutions who are involved in that fraud and manipulation. I recognize that these are serious charges on my part, and I do not make them lightly.

Allow me to explain myself, in the simplest words I can muster. Keep in mind, I am aware of no establishment voice that confirms my contention that leasing/forward selling of gold and silver is inherently dishonest. I think that is because this leasing/forward selling business has become so entrenched that even those who see the picture correctly, are reluctant to speak up. The only confirmation I seek here is that of the reader's common sense.

The first thing you must do, in order to understand gold and silver leasing, is to take the word "lease", and throw it out the window. I believe that the very word is at the heart of the misunderstanding about metal leasing. Because, in gold and silver leasing, what actually takes place bears no resemblance to any other type of lease you have experienced. When you hear the word "lease", the logical response is that something is being "borrowed" for a fee. At the termination of the lease, that which is borrowed is returned. That's what the word lease means. There are very few people in the US who have not participated in a lease. It is that ingrained experience, that causes the misunderstanding in gold and silver leases.

The difference between metals leasing and all other types of leasing is the "return" part. We all know that the item being leased must be returned or accounted for. And, to be sure, even in gold and silver leasing there is a stated contractual obligation to return any gold and silver loaned. But, here is where you must rely on your common sense and determine if what I am alleging is true. Something happens in every single gold and silver loan, at the outset of the transaction, that renders the whole concept of metals leasing as fraudulent. That something is that the collateral of a metals loan, the actual metal itself, is sold (or consumed) and thereby destroyed. That is the big difference. It is the main point. What kind of secured lease permits the security to be purchased by an unrelated third party? Yet, that is precisely what happens in every single gold and silver lease.

Look at it this way. If you owned a condominium, and decided to lease it out, in return for rent paid to you, you would hope and expect the tenant to maintain the property in decent shape. You wouldn't expect him to trash it. One thing you certainly would not expect the tenant to do would be to sell your condo to someone else, and pocket the proceeds, even if the tenant promised to return your condo, or pay you back someday in the future. That would be preposterous. Outrageous! Illegal! Fraudulent! Yet that is precisely what happens in every gold and silver loan.

Because of this outrageous conveyance of property, metal loans are inherently fraudulent. And manipulative. It doesn't matter who is participating in these loans. What matters is that the process itself and very nature of these metal loans is fraudulent, thereby tainting those who participate. If someone is involved in a metal loan, then they are automatically involved in widespread fraud and manipulation.

OK, so what exactly are these gold and silver loans, and who is involved? Remember, I'm trying to keep this simple and accurate. The big lenders are the Central Banks of various countries. The big borrowers are the gold miners (in silver, the list of borrowers is broader). The Bullion Banks serve as the middlemen. The Bullion Banks are household names – JP Morgan (Chase), Goldman Sachs, AIG, Bank of Nova Scotia and others. The scheme works like this. Central Banks, with their large holdings of gold and silver, "lend" metal to the Bullion Banks, who in turn, extract a promise to repay the Central Banks metal from mining companies out of future production. The mining companies get to sell or use the metal until the time of repayment. The key to the whole scheme is that the Central Banks offer their metal out on loan, for the lowest known interest rate in the Western World, typically one half to one percent per annum. Without that artificial low interest rate, gold and silver loans would not and could not exist. The first proof that these loans are rotten to the core is that the Central Banks, by accepting such a low return on their metal, are doing something unnatural, namely they are accepting less than what they could get. The Central Banks are in the driver's seat. They could charge the bullion bankers any interest rate they choose, yet they accept a half and one percent per annum interest, where they could charge 10%. After all, what could the borrowers do?

The borrowers still have to return metal collateral that doesn't exist. The Central Banks have the borrowers over a barrel, yet they only ask for 1%. More crazy than this, is hard to imagine. Here we have loans that can't possibly be paid off collectively, and only 1% is accepted.

Everyone knows that a secured mortgage on a home is at least 7%. Where do they get off charging 1% on a completely unsecured loan? In fact, the metal leases are worse than an unsecured loan because the currency with which they have to pay it back doesn't exist.

Ask yourself this - how can an inert, basic material even throw off an interest rate, in the first place? Why any interest rate? This is the heart of the whole fraud. Metals can't return an interest rate under any condition. Period. Let me repeat that - metals can't possibly generate interest. Even though you may see offers for "interest " on gold and silver, it isn't real interest that is being earned, it is something else. Just like the word "lease" is incorrectly used to describe what is really a sale, "interest" is a misleading word. This is not "interest", this is something entirely different. This is a fee paid by the Bullion Banks to the Central Banks for the physical transfer of their metal. It can't be called a legitimate sale because only 1% of the proceeds is payable over the course of a whole year, and not the full value of the metal transferred. What it comes down to is this. The Central Banks are trusting the Bullion Banks to return something that can't be returned and are accepting a 1% fee per year for this "privilege". That everyone accepts this Ponzi arrangement as a legitimate "loan with interest" is preposterous.

I don't equivocate when I say these gold and silver loans can't be paid back. Let me prove it to you. Oh, of course, some individual gold and silver loans are paid back, or rearranged from time to time. But, they can't be paid back collectively. In fact, 99% of these loans are short term (one month to one year), and are automatically rolled over.

They are always rolled over. They have to be because they can't be paid back. Here's why. Since the old loans are always rolled over, and because new loans are constantly being created, there is a cumulative effect to these loans. They just keep growing and growing. It is generally accepted that a minimum of two years worth of world mine production is what these gold and silver loans have grown to. What this means is that, in order to pay these loans off, two full years of world mine production would be required.

Metal was borrowed, metal must be repaid. Two full years' worth. Think about that. Think about how it could be possible for the world to take two full years of world gold and silver production, and set it aside to pay off these stupid, stupid loans. You have to imagine, for two long years a world with no new jewelry, no photography, no electronics. You can't imagine that. That is impossible. Yes, that is why it is impossible for these loans to be paid back. And if you have a whole class of loans that can be proven, by common sense, to be impossible to be paid back, wouldn't you consider that to be fraud? Wouldn't you consider anyone engaged in granting new loans, or rolling over old loans, to be engaged in a fraud, wittingly or unwittingly?

But that's only one of many proofs that gold and silver leasing is fraudulent and manipulative. Think about this. Leasing something allows you to use something for a fee. How in the world does someone "use" a bar of gold or silver? As a doorstop? There are only two ways you can "use" a bar of metal. Sell it or melt it. Period. Please think about this. If all you can do with a bar of metal, is sell it or melt it, how could such an item be leased in the first place? Only things that can legitimately be used can be leased. Money, cars, homes, machinery, airplanes, computers, even people themselves (contract workers), can be leased, because there is a utility value to each. But how can you lease an inert, non-utilitarian basic material? You can't, legitimately. All you can do with such an item is sell it, or consume it. The simple point here is this - everyone is calling these gold and silver transactions leases, but that's hogwash. They are sales, pure and simple. And if a financial transaction is intentionally mislabeled, in order to conceal its true nature, how can that not be some kind of fraud?

You see, since the only "use" one can derive from a bar of gold or silver is a sale or melt, all gold and silver loans are really sales or consumption. The metal that the Central Banks "loan" actually leaves the Central Banks vaults, and is sold by the Bullion Bankers to convert the metal into something useful - cash. You didn't think anyone would actually "borrow" metal just to hold it and keep it secure, did you? That would make no sense. And, because the Central banks are selling, not loaning, we hit upon another fraudulent feature to these transactions.

That is, the Central Banks, by lending, are really selling massive amounts of gold and silver, and are not reporting those sales. Because the disappearance of real metal from the vaults of the Central Banks is not being reported, the Central Banks who participate in gold loans have much less in their vaults than they publicly claim. That's fraudulent reporting. The Central Banks will claim that they don't have to report the actual metal missing from their vaults, because they are technically classified as "loans". They're lying through their teeth. It is criminal, as far as I can tell. (Silver is not considered monetary, so the Central Banks don't report any sales or "loan" sales.) So, when you see the official holdings of a Central Bank, if they are engaged in these metal loans, their books are cooked. They have less than they are reporting. It's terrible.

45

But, the fraudulent reporting of phantom metal holdings, as bad as it is, is not the worst thing. The worst thing, by far, is the economic effect these loans have had on the price of gold and silver. It has decimated the price of each. Because these loans are really sales, real metal is dumped on the market when the loan is originated. And dump is too kind a word. There are a minimum of 150 million ounces of gold, and one billion ounces of silver, out on "loan" from the Central Banks. That means that over the past 10 years or so, 15 million ounces of gold, and 100 million ounces of silver have been sold each year, on average, as a result of these loans. Since the loans are never paid back, this is all extra supply. This is in addition to mine production, recycling and straight Central Bank sales. Think of it this way, since we have annual world mine production of roughly 75 million ounces of gold, and 500 million ounces of silver, gold and silver loans have dumped two full years of world mine production on the market. How could prices not go down, and stay down with that type of extra supply? Think of any commodity that you want. Imagine someone dumping two full years of production onto the market. In a free market, a change of 5% or 10% in supply or demand sends most commodities to price extremes. Now imagine 200%. It's a wonder that gold and silver are not lower. This is the manipulation and fraud of all time.

There are no real defenders of metal leasing, the premise is too stupid. Let's face it, if it wasn't as fraudulent and manipulative as I claim, then folks would be able to poke holes in what I say. They don't, because they can't. But the purpose of this article is not to recite the evils of gold and silver leasing. The purpose is to explain to you just what has really been going on in the gold and silver markets for a positive and constructive goal.

Let's face it, I have established a documented track record claiming fraud and manipulation in gold and silver. I don't need to add to that documentation. My purpose here is to explain to you how you can profit from this outrageous situation. You know, when you're given lemons, make lemonade. The upside to the ongoing manipulation of these fraudulent gold and silver loans is the once in a lifetime opportunity that today's depressed prices offer. Were it not for these gold and silver loans dumping massive quantities of metal on the market, prices would be nowhere near where we are right now. This is an unintended consequence of the manipulation of gold and silver loans. Unintended, because the purpose of this whole loan experiment was, obviously, not to present you with the buy point of a lifetime. That's just the way it has turned out.

What's important for you to do, is to think this leasing business through, and if you decide I am right, to position yourself the best way possible to take advantage of the unraveling of this stupid idea. That is one thing I can almost guarantee you. This leasing will eventually be exposed for the fraud it is. The end will come suddenly, because all frauds end that way. What you have to do is to position yourself beforehand, and to make sure you are in the right vehicle. The choices are many and the pitfalls will be great. This 20-year experiment in lending something that can't be lent is coming to an end. The end will be violent. There will be an upheaval in the gold and silver world that has never been witnessed before. No one, certainly not I, can pinpoint with accuracy all the effects of this upheaval. But, it's going to be big, and it's going to be bad. If you are positioned wrong, you can lose.

It's no secret that my favorite play is real silver. I'm just trying to play it safe. I don't think it is a time to try to be clever and take chances. If there were no such thing as silver, I would go with gold. But, there is such a thing as silver, so silver it is. I believe that will give you the biggest, surest bang for your buck. Gold comes next. All paper contracts are suspect. Leverage should be avoided unless you are a dyed in the wool gambler, and are feeling real lucky. This isn't a mining company forum, but if you pick a miner who is short (has promised to pay back-borrowed metal), a price rise could be disastrous, as it was to Ashanti and Cambior in the gold spike of September 1999. If you're undecided on what to choose, keep it simple. Buy real silver. Don't let the bluff of even lower manipulated prices throw you off the track. Use it to your advantage. Not only do you have the lease scam working in your favor, you have the added bonus of buying an item in critical shortage. Just keep in mind that the trick is to buy it before the leasing fraud is extinguished. To pass Leasing 101, you must be prepared for the final exam. There will be no "make-ups" offered. Good luck.

Chapter 5

Commodity Trading and Price Effects

Some readers will know that for several years I have been a commentator on the Financial Sense News Hour, see www.financialsense.com. This website is brought to the public by Puplava Securities and the internet radio shows are hosted by one of the most highly respected financial experts in the world today. Jim Puplava has in my view given the investing public more truthful information on the actual status of the economic system from a world perspective than anyone else I could name.

The following article is from Mr. Puplava and will instill in the reader some of the most important points about how the paper markets operate. Later in this chapter we will explore some other thoughts on the precious metals trading by way of the commodity markets.

Paper Rules
by Jim Puplava.

The paper markets control the commodity markets regardless of the size of the market. Through the use of derivatives, a small amount of capital controls the commodity markets worldwide. That amount is estimated to be somewhere in the neighborhood of around $200 billion.

This is a highly geared market where a small amount of capital controls a much larger market. In this case, it is $200 billion in actual cash money that is leveraged to the tenth degree through paper contracts that control a trillion dollar market for hard commodities ranging from oil to gold. In "Debt & Delusion," Peter Warburton has made a strong case for how central banks have waged war against tangible assets in order to keep their prices suppressed. This is done through gearing the commodity markets whereby a small amount of capital is leveraged into a position of control over a much larger market.

This gearing process, which is facilitated through the use of derivatives, allows sophisticated investors, hedge funds and investment houses in the US and in Europe to control the commodity markets and various asset classes by driving their prices to levels that distort their fundamental equilibrium price. In other words, what we see in commodities is not their fair market value price as determined by free markets. Instead, we see an artificial price determined by paper contracts. This perceived market price is in fact a gross distortion of actual demand fundamentals. Prices have been kept artificially low for so long a period of time; it has given the illusion that there is no inflation. What is not measured or considered in this proposition is that the inflation has taken place in the paper markets as reflected in the current price of paper assets such as stocks, bonds, and currencies. Low commodity prices, which have been kept low by gearing, are always shown as evidence that there are no signs of inflation.

Gearing Distorts Markets

This whole artificial process of paper market distortion of the commodity markets has allowed prices to deteriorate at the same time that demand has risen and supply has contracted. Prices have been kept low; while demand for products has expanded. This runs contrary to general economic laws of supply and demand. Demand increases, supplies contract and the price of a commodity falls.

The fact that nobody questions this is even more astounding. While demand has risen, the supply of particular commodities has fallen off due to disinvestments, divestiture and the general contraction of most commodity-like businesses. Supplies and reserves accumulated over decades have been drawn down in order to meet supply deficits. The gasoline in your car probably came from an oil well that was discovered 25 years ago in the US and over 40 years ago in the Middle East. The silver that is used in your camera is coming from the sale of scrap silver and the depletion of above-ground inventories. Gold deficits are made up from central bank sales and gold leasing. This consumption of aboveground stockpiles of commodities accumulated over decades cannot last forever.

As inventory levels from natural gas, oil, silver, gold and other commodities are drawn down, a supply train wreck or price shock is slowly building momentum. Already we are facing our second oil price shock in three years. Oil prices have been distorted by a combination of political convolutions and derivatives. Once supply stockpiles are depleted, prices will reverse and head higher as demand fundamentals and a loss of confidence in paper overwhelm commodity markets. One day soon Americans and the West in general are going to wake up to find the financial world and the commodity markets aren't, as they seem. Supply shortages of key commodities, energy outages and other supply disruptions should become more commonplace. In the case of silver, gold, oil and natural gas, we will see prices rise to their true fundamental value, which by the way is much higher than what is now reflected in the markets.

Short Positions Distort Bullion & Share Prices

A good example of this is the silver markets were short positions on the COMEX and short positions in key silver stocks have acted to suppress the price of the metal and key silver stocks far below their intrinsic value. The following table below shows the growth in short positions in silver stocks that have doubled, tripled, and in some cases quadrupled since May of this year. These short positions have been the key, along with short positions on the COMEX in silver, to keeping the price of silver and silver stock prices suppressed. Yet, nothing has changed fundamentally in the business. According to CPM Group, the silver deficit will be larger this year than last year. And despite a recession and weakening economies across the globe, silver deficits last year were close to 80 million.

Short Changing The Silver Market: Short Interest on Settlement Date

I recently met with the head CEO of a silver mining company who has been able to increase the reserves of his company significantly over the last four months adding real value for his shareholders. And yet his stock has been sold short and driven down in half as a result of a huge short position. I know most of the key owners of this company and very strong hands hold it. The float is narrow and the short position would take at least 3-4 days to cover at present volume. Nothing has changed fundamentally that would warrant such a short position.

There are very few large silver mines in the world in comparison to gold. And silver stockpiles are running out. At the present rate of deficit, there is approximately 1-2 years left in above-ground stockpiles (not counting silver coins). Pure silver mines are rare since most silver is mined as a by-product of other metals. About 80 percent of the supply of silver comes to the market as a by-product of other base metals. Pure silver companies can be counted on two hands. Silver, as a commodity, is getting rarer even as demand and use for silver increases. Why do you thing Buffett bought silver back in 1997 and still holds on to it? Why have Gates, Soros, Tish, and others bought silver? There is a reason. They think the price of silver is going up. It is becoming a rare commodity in that it is harder to find; while supplies dwindle. Its price is kept down artificially by huge short positions. Note the chart to the right which graphically depicts the total short position noted in the table above.

Investment Philosophy Determines Position

There are two ways in which to look at this situation: one negative and one positive. It all depends on your investment philosophy. If you're a short-term trader, you can skip this part because it will be of no use to you. You can trade into the stocks or metal when it explodes at much higher prices. If you are a value investor and think long-term, you have an opportunity that has been handed to you. You have the chance to accumulate shares of only a handful of pure silver companies in the world at bargain prices. The shorts in effect are subsidizing your investment purchases. I have always used these kinds of opportunities to buy at someone else's expense. As prices head lower, as short positions increase, I can use the opportunity to buy key mining companies, in my case just two, at much lower prices. The shorts will have to cover, and when they do, the very narrowness of the market in pure silver companies will explode. You can see this in the price of the shares back in May, June, and July. As other buyers came into the market, the price of silver mining shares exploded before forming a double top and heading down as short interest increased.

If you are a believer in this metal, based on strong long-term fundamentals, then you are now afforded the opportunity to accumulate shares at much lower prices. Or if you own them, you can acquire additional shares at much lower prices and significantly add to your position. Of course this philosophy only applies to believers in silver's fundamentals and investors who think strategically and outside the box.

Investment success doesn't come easy. If it did, we would all be millionaires. Success comes from hard work, a right attitude and the development of an investment philosophy. Going along with the crowd and the consensus will lead you down the path to mediocrity and below-average returns. Just think of what you been have told by Wall Street and most analysts and economists. You have been told to buy and hold even as they trade, short, and sell. Think of what their advice has brought you. Look at long-term charts of silver, gold, oil, and natural gas. Look at how these markets have performed, then look at your S&P Index fund or your mutual fund and draw your own conclusions. One of these markets is emerging as the new bull on the Street and the other is dissipating in a protracted bear market. Which side of the fence are you on? Isn't it time to cross over to the other side of the street?

You have been afforded another opportunity to buy, buy when prices are cheap. You have also been given another opportunity to sell. Don't listen to the media or Wall Street analysts or economists. They have steered you wrong for the last three years. How many more years do you want to experience the pains of a bear market before most of your hard earned savings are eaten away? Do your own homework, look at the charts and get wisdom and understanding. If you don't have the time, then find someone who does. More importantly, take responsibility for your own finances. This is not the time to play ostrich and bury your head in the sand. Storms are swirling all around you and it is time to get prepared.

Today's Market

Speaking of storms, stocks fell for the fourth day out of five as more earnings warnings turned a short rally into a rout. The financial sector accounted for most of the losses as more financial institutions report lower earnings as a result of bad loans. The plunge in financial stocks indicate that more bad earnings reports will surface in the weeks ahead. Today it was the Bank of New York, which reported a profit shortfall due to bad loans. Shares of bank and financial companies accounted for 80 percent of the drop in the S&P 500. The S&P 500 is now down 29 percent for the year heading for its third consecutive year of losses. The Dow has lost 23 percent this year; while the NASDAQ continues to hemorrhage with a YTD loss of 40 percent. Analysts continue to cut their pro forma earnings forecast for the third quarter down to 6.3 percent.

The financial sector, once considered a safe haven from the stock market storms, is now showing signs of stress as one financial institution after another report greater loan losses. Defaults, bankruptcies, and delinquencies are all in a sharp uptrend as a result of an over leveraged corporate and consumer sector.

Chapter 6

Is Silver Money?
"The major monetary metal in history is silver, not gold."
Nobel Laureate Milton Friedman

Silver has the six aspects of money in a classical sense. It is divisible, durable, convenient, consistent, has utility value, and cannot be created by fiat. Silver is used as a medium of exchange and as a store of value.

First, it is a recorded fact that silver has been used in more places and for longer periods of time as money than gold. It is impossible to write about silver without evoking emotions, although it is my goal to be as objective as possible. There are very strong views about this metal both positive and negative. One such area involves the silver as money issue. The facts are that precious metals are rare, fiat currencies can be printed at will, and have always been abused.

We all have a vested interest in the monetary system holding together. Precious metals are a barometer of world financial health. If gold and silver start moving up in a manner similar to 1979-1980, then the paper money game is essentially finished. Will this happen? Objectively, I do not know! However, I do know, throughout all of recorded history when a country has adopted a monetary system founded on edict (fiat), the nation has had financial problems. As we enter the next century, remember the gold window was closed in 1971 and for the first time in history, the reserve fiat currency is worldwide phenomena.

The price of silver is a function of understanding the market itself. When the market understands that money based on unsound principles cannot help but fail eventually, then the true value of silver will be determined. Until that time arrives it is prudent to prepare some savings in the form that best retains value.

It would be of tremendous importance to everyone if I were able to predict one event in the investment world that had a 100% certainty of being fulfilled. I cannot, however here is something to ponder. Most fiat currencies have eventually reached their intrinsic value of zero. This implies that many currencies around the world may reach zero as well.

The source of all wealth is land. If you believe God created the Earth fine, if not fine, we all can agree we live in a physical universe and land composes part of the Earth's character. Let me repeat myself, the source of all wealth is land. That is an interesting concept is it not? Gold and silver are mined out of the earth, many foodstuffs are grown in soil, houses, apartments, and shopping centers are built on it. In fact most of the list of commodities are derived from the land in one way or another, from soybeans to cotton, from sugar to copper. However, there is one subset that trades on the commodities exchanges that are the sole creation of man- fiat currencies, bonds, notes, and bills. In todays world "money" created out of nothing.

The world has entered into a great economic shift from paper assets to hard assets. This cycle repeats itself and now is the time when investors should be or should have shifted their holding to underweight in stocks and bonds and begun to accumulate physical commodity type assets.

Now we have some insight into where we are in the economic cycle between paper assets and physical assets. What takes place at the end of great inflations? What does history teach us? Actually, at the end of the inflation two interesting things happen.

First, real money begins to appear in the market for everyday transactions. Almost anyone on the Internet is aware gold can and is used for transactions through various gold backed Internet currencies. There are also some actual warehouse receipts being used such as the Liberty Dollar and Millennium Money. These warehouse receipts are exchangeable by the bearer on demand for actual silver or gold. The receipts themselves can also be used to purchase everyday items.

The second issue is that man-made instruments are exchanged for real wealth at an accelerating rate during periods of uncertainty. The problem is that once this transfer begins there are not many places to find safety. Because money represents something that can be used presently or stored for future use this shift becomes very intriguing. Although the major shift is into commodities, which of the commodities are able to fulfill the ability to be spent presently or store value for future use?

Yes, land and real estate can and will be used, but land is not very liquid. The only real place to transfer the financial asset class that provides safety, liquidity, and a store of value, is the precious metals.

The Significance & Sanity of Silver as Money

"We are completely dependent on the commercial banks. Someone has to borrow every dollar we have in circulation, cash or credit. If

the banks create ample synthetic money, we are prosperous; if not, we starve. We are absolutely without a permanent money system. When one gets a complete grasp of the picture, the tragic absurdity of our hopeless position is almost incredible, but there it is. It is the most important subject intelligent persons can investigate and reflect upon. It is so important that our present civilization may collapse unless it becomes widely understood and the defects remedied soon."
– Robert H. Hemphill, *Credit Manager of the Federal Reserve Bank, Atlanta, GA*

This article is about silver's monetary role throughout history, though it should be read as an overview since much more complete works exist on this subject. It is truly impossible to discuss silver as money without mentioning gold's role as well. At times countries have been on a gold standard or a silver standard or a dual standard. My aim with this piece is to encourage readers to consider the role they believe silver has in today's economy. Is silver a monetary metal? Is it an industrial commodity? Is it both?

In this brief preface, two ideas are pertinent to all. First, the above quote from Robert Hemphill will be meaningful to you only if YOU give it meaning. To wit, only when you are able to prove to your own satisfaction that a debt-based monetary system poses no threat to your financial well being and will be able to endure through your children's lifetime will you feel secure. Second, consider how you might protect yourself if you turn out to be wrong. In other words, if you were to allocate a mere 5% of your investment portfolio to silver, just how badly could you be hurt? Sure, if silver were to go to zero, you'd lose 5% of your total investment base – but, were silver to reach its former highs, your small allocation might prove a highly welcome asset in a not-so-certain world. With this background let us begin.

Economists seem as a whole to be totally perplexed by money. Even free market economists usually insist that some sort of government control is needed for money. These same economists seldom consider that government control of money is interference in the free market! Historically, money was one of the first things controlled by government. In my opinion, however, the free market is best at determining money.

Gold and Silver are Assets, Not Liabilities

An argument often mentioned about gold is that it is the only asset that is not simultaneously someone else's liability. This is fiction not fact. Silver, copper, iron, or even cotton, tobacco, or cornmeal would be able to perform the same function. In other words, nearly any commodity that is totally owned by someone is an asset and not a liability.

Many different goods have been used as money throughout history. Throughout centuries, only two commodities, gold and silver, have emerged as money in the free competition of the market, and have displaced the other commodities. In a free market, people and their economic interactions develop the medium of exchange. This is what establishes what money is. Government calling bits of paper "money" does not establish it. The most important truth is thus established; MONEY IS A COMMODITY! "Learning this simple lesson is one of the world's most important tasks. So often have people talked about money as something much more or less than this. Money is not an abstract unit of account, divorceable from a concrete good; it is not a useless token only good for exchanging;

61

it is not a 'claim on society"; it is not a guarantee of a fixed price level. It is simply a commodity. It differs from other commodities in being demanded mainly as a medium of exchange." 1

The shape of the money unit makes no difference. If copper is the money for example, then all copper is money, whether it is a pipe, chunk, bar, coin, or picture frame. This is not to say that some shapes are not more convenient than others. The free market will determine if a coin is to carry a premium over another form of the same metal.

Another area that can be simplified is the money supply question. It cannot be estimated how much effort and nonsense has been written on this subject. The question is really how much money does the world need? Can the free market determine the correct amount of money? For this illustration let us use one commodity established by the free market as money. For this example I will use silver. The first point is that the money supply is the total weight of silver existing. Changes in the money supply would be determined by the same factors as other goods. Increases would come from increased mine supply and decreases from being used up by wear and tear, industry, or loss. So, what should the money supply be? Only a few have suggested the obvious, let the market itself decide.

Money Is Different

Money differs from all other commodities and this difference must be fully understood. When the supply of any other good increases, this is beneficial as more goods mean an increased standard of living. Consumer goods are used up, capital goods are used up, but money is not used up. Its function remains and it is still available for further transactions. Let us suppose for example that we were able to double the money supply (amount of silver), would we be twice as rich? Absolutely not, what makes one rich is an abundance of goods. What limits that abundance is a scarcity of land, labor, or capital. Thus, an increase in the supply of silver only dilutes the worth of each ounce, whereas a fall in supply raises the power of each silver ounce to do its work. "We come to the startling truth that it does not matter what the supply of money is. Any supply will do as well as any other supply."2 The free market will simply adjust by changing the purchasing power or effectiveness of the silver unit.

Gold & Silver were used as money in ancient civilizations including BC Rome. The first reference I could find to money was in Genesis 44:8 – "Behold, the money, which we found in our sacks' mouths, we brought again unto thee out of the land of Canaan: how then should we steal out of thy lord's house silver or gold?" The first monetary transaction recorded in the Bible is also in Genesis. Abraham weighs 400 shekels of silver to pay for his wife's burial. This is the same Abraham all three major religions of the world express as a link to the God in which they believe. Judaism, Christianity and Islam all refer to the "God of Abraham." This reference to silver in Genesis applies universally, across cultures, and throughout the ages.

Silver has had a monetary function far longer than gold, being used as the most common medium of exchange in everyday commerce since well before the time of Christ. In this article, my aim is to promote an understanding that silver retains a vital monetary purpose and is, in fact, more crucial to mankind than ever before. This is true both financially and socially – financially because of the problems associated with a fiat money system and socially because silver is crucial to our modern way of life.

Three metals have a history of monetary usage – gold, silver and copper. Silver has been most useful because gold is simply too rare for common daily transactions. Gold has been reserved primarily for final payment in large bank-to-bank or nation-to-nation dealings. Copper has been used mainly as a medium for very small exchanges. (As an interesting sidelight, note that even copper is debased out of the currency system in periods of extreme inflation. The U.S. government now makes the penny with a zinc alloy because it was losing money on the minting of copper pennies.)

Silver IS Money

Indeed, silver's monetary role has been so universally recognized throughout history that the very word for silver is money in many languages. In Italian, Spanish and French the words for "money" and "silver" can be interchanged. In Hebrew, the word kesepph means both silver and money. Even in early American slang, the word silver was often used to signify payment: "Grease my palm with silver!" To be precise, among more than 250 million people in 51 countries, the word for money is identical to the word for silver. Many Europeans refer to both silver and money as "argent," while Spanish-speaking people the world over use "plata" to mean silver, money or both.

Before moving ahead, it might be interesting to look back for a moment. The following was written over two decades ago, but still deserves careful contemplation. "Most of the gold that has been mined from the ground is now stored in the ground – in bank vaults. Industrial demand for gold today, even though it is growing, is small compared to existing stocks. Consequently, within our lifetime – and possibly within this decade –silver could become more valuable ounce-for-ounce than gold. Of course, both will become more valuable in terms of paper money by a large multiple because of the accelerating and uncontrollable worldwide paper-money inflation that lies ahead."3

As I've noted before, this is beyond what I expect. However, the current relative values for gold and silver should definitely favor silver in the long term.

A Brief Review of Silver's Recent Monetary History

Silver was the primary commercial money for most of the world's people from earliest recorded history until the past century. Silver price for most of the 19th century was fixed at the coinage value of $1.29 per troy ounce. During the great silver boom of the 1860s, which vastly expanded the silver supply, the world became flooded with silver coinage.

Another key point in silver's monetary history came during deflation, devaluation and Depression of the 1930s. Silver's price fell lower and lower, finally bottoming at 25 cents in 1933. However, the Thomas Act of 1933 allowed foreign debtors to pay the U.S. in silver coin at 50 cents per ounce, twice the unofficial price, and silver soon strengthened worldwide. The price rallied to 44 cents by the end of 1933, a 75% increase above the Depression low, but it could still be said that silver was clearly in a state of monetary confusion. (The Thomas Act also authorized a reduction in the gold content of the U.S. dollar. At the request of insolvent bankers, all banks were closed, an embargo was put on gold sales and the dollar was allowed to float.)

The next major monetary adjustment for silver resulted from another political action. The Silver Purchase Act of 1934 directed the Secretary of the Treasury to purchase silver both at home and abroad until the market price reached the official monetary price of $1.29 per ounce. This political action quickly inspired still another political action. The U.S. Treasury issued an edict that taxed domestic silver transactions at 50 percent in order "to capture the windfall profits created by the Treasury." Over the next four years, the U.S. acquired 3.2 billion ounces of silver – including the physical confiscation of so much actual silver stock that it became impossible for the Commodity Exchange of New York (Comex) to function.

From 1934 until 1955, the Treasury support price for silver remained above the actual market price. After 1955, however, the market price began to exceed the Treasury price, with silver users (largely in the photographic and electronics fields) buying silver from both domestic mines and the Treasury.

Faced with dwindling supplies and increasing market prices for silver, the Coinage Act of 1965 moved through Congress, boosted by a letter dated June 3, 1965, from President Lyndon Johnson, which declared his support for the elimination of silver from coinage in the United States. "There is no dependable or likely prospect that new, economically workable sources of silver may be found that could appreciably narrow the gap between silver supply and demand," Johnson wrote. "The optimistic outlook is for an increase of about 20 percent over the next four years. This would be of little help. Further, because silver is produced chiefly as a by-product of the mining of copper, lead and zinc, even a very large increase in the price of silver would not stimulate silver production sufficiently to change the outlook."[4]

Significant Points About Real Money and Silver

First, silver again lasted longer than gold as a medium of exchange (real money), surviving until 1965, whereas gold ceased to circulate among people in the US in 1933, being reserved for balance-of-trade payments until the gold window was closed in 1971.

Second, to properly understand what President Johnson did, you need to know something about the rule of law. A contract is sacred and cannot be broken – but Johnson essentially urged Congress to break the contract with the American people that's printed on all silver certificates. Some Americans, aware of what was really going on, saved every 90%-silver coin they could get their hands on.

Third, it is a total fallacy that there is too little gold or silver left for it to be used as money. This is something I hear over and over – and it is completely erroneous. The correct observation is that too many paper claims have been issued against the currently existing amount of real money.

Finally, in a true gold standard, many financial planners would be out of business. As absurd as this sounds, follow the logic. If the monetary system were based on honest weights and measures, you would know, when you first entered the work force at, say, 20 years of age, exactly how much you would need to save by age 65 for retirement. Why? Because your purchasing power would remain constant. Under an honest monetary system, interest rates are stable and long-range planning is simplified. In a true gold standard, purchasing power actually increases slightly over time so that an ounce of gold would buy slightly more after 35 years than it did when you originally entered the work force.

Obviously, a true gold standard is not perfect, and there are still problems associated with human interaction. The potential buying power of gold has importance for determining silver's usage as money. For example, if gold reaches a price in U.S. dollars of $2,000 per ounce, then the smallest practical coins, being the one-tenth ounce pieces, would have a value of roughly $200. This is far too large for a great many daily transactions – e.g., buying bread, milk or gasoline. If coins were to be used in commerce, they might revert back to gold, silver, and copper.

Moving back to the theme of synthetic (fiat) money, problems compound one upon another. Holders of the U.S. debt become restless and irritable being forced to pile up dollars that are now starting to lose value relative to their currency. As the purchasing power of dollar falls, they become increasingly unwanted by foreign governments. But they are locked into a system that offers little in the way of relief. The long running problem (we have almost finished the race) is that these other countries will not sit by forever and watch their currencies become more expensive and their exports hurt for the benefit of America. As the dollar depreciates further, there will be competition.

This could lead to exchange controls, currency blocs, and all types of economic warfare. In a strategic move during the current global tensions, some countries are exchanging U.S. debt for gold. This has an effect upon America because as the U.S. loses its dominance in the financial markets prestige and power wane as well.

It's Time for Re-Evaluation

In conclusion, I must agree that money is the most important subject intelligent persons can investigate and reflect upon. Our civilization stands at a very important point. Many are looking at the leadership not only on the political front, but also on the corporate level. Scandals are daily news, the dollar has come under attack, and "money" has disappeared from many investor portfolios. Is your monetary future based on facts, mere faith – or total fiction?

Footnotes

1) *Rothbard, Murray, What Has Government Done To Our Money, Praxeology Press, Auburn, Alabama, 1990, p.19.*
2) *Ibid., p.30-31.*
3) *Smith, Jerome, Silver Profits in The Eighties, ERC Publishing, New York, NY, 1982, p.xvi.*
4) *Johnson, President Lyndon, Letter to The Congress, June 3, 1965.*

Chapter 7

New uses for Silver and Coming Demand Squeeze

By now, everyone should be aware of the on-going energy problems faced by the world. What if I were to tell you there is a very viable solution to help the current energy situation? What if this positive solution was ready to implement - and, once it's in place, it would be the most efficient movement of electricity ever known to mankind.

What I'm talking about relates to a problem known as "line loss." Specifically, when electricity is generated, not all the power reaches the end user. A large percentage of it is simply eroded away by the resistance it encounters in the lines through which it is transmitted. In fact, this "line loss" sometimes runs in excess of 30 percent. However, there is a method that, for practical purposes, can reduce the line loss to almost nothing. It involves a technology called superconductivity.

I first became interested in this technology after reading a backgrounder prepared by the Silver Institute. In researching the technology, I discovered there is a company that now has it fully in place the American Superconductor Corporation (ASC). ASC's corporate profile reads as follows:

"American Superconductor Corporation is a world leader in developing and manufacturing products utilizing super-conducting materials and power electronic devices for electric power applications.

American Superconductor's products - and those sold by electrical equipment manufacturers that incorporate its products - can dramatically increase the capacity and reliability of power-delivery networks, significantly reduce manufacturing costs for electrical equipment such as motors and generators, lower operating costs and conserve resources used to generate electric power. Founded in 1987, the company is headquartered in Westborough, Mass. For more information, visit www.amsuper.com."

That obviously sounds great for the power-hungry people of the world but the question for us now becomes, "What does this have to do with silver?"

The answer is: Everything!

According to the Silver Institute backgrounder, the super-conductivity technology requires silver for the super-conducting transmission line. At this point in time the amount of silver to be used in this new technology is not known, however estimates from the Silver Institute indicate that perhaps as much as 50 million ounces of silver per year could be used in this application alone.

Despite that caution, however, the prospects for super-conductivity still strongly reinforce my contention - which is simple. There's absolutely no evidence of an impending drop in industrial demand for silver in fact it seems more and more uses are being developed all the time.

An area that we are perhaps the first to examine is that of the Radio Frequency Identification chip, commonly known as RFID. We received this a short time ago:

I recently stumbled over the use of silver in the production of RFID's. Common RFID's can be scanned / received only up to 5 meters which is not enough for efficient storage management. Next generation RFID's will have a silver antenna and cover a distance of up to 15 meters. Silver can be mangled, rolled, thinned out, second to gold only. A silver antenna can be folded many times, is longer and smaller and therefore fits perfectly. That's a small amount of silver in these chips that is irrecoverable you get the story. Add to this the expected go ahead from the ISO (International Standardization Organization) for RFID's in November and it should really give the metal a boost.

Our preliminary research into this area produced some rather startling results. The minimum use of silver for a single RFID is 1/100 of a gram of silver. However, our sources indicate that by 2008 about 100 billion RFID's will be produced on an annual basis. This would produce a consumption rate of over 30 million ounces of silver annually, and most of this silver would end up in the waste dumps. This is greater than the amount of silver that will be produced annually by San Cristobal, Apex's large zinc/silver mine.

Remember you read it here first, but we need to also address the implications of this chip. This small device could destroy personal liberty and privacy. The chip's ID number is relayed to the reader, which identifies the item and its history. This technology is going to be big business very soon. As reported in RFIDNews, "With major companies planning to increase the deployment and integration of RFID systems in retail stores and warehouses in the years ahead, the market for related consulting, implementation, and managed services is expected to grow by 47% in 2004 and reach Euro 1.5 billion worldwide by 2008."

Wal-Mart is especially eager to make RFID technology mandatory among all of its suppliers. The General Services Administration stated they are, "encouraged to consider action that can be taken to advance the industry by demonstrating the long-term intent of the agency to adopt RFID technological solutions."

It is interesting to note that the more technology driven by culture the more silver is used per person. As China continues to modernize more and more silver will be demanded. At the present time the Chinese use approximately 1/70th the amount of silver per capita that is used in North America. This obviously leaves a huge potential demand increase from China as the wealth of that nation increases.

As China builds its infrastructure, more and more silver will be needed. From 1998 until 2003, China reported that their internal mining activity was meeting their demand for silver. In fact, China has reported exporting silver in those years. However, in 2004, the total mining activity in China did not meet their requirements. Having spent time with both the official Chinese Silver Delegation and top officials at the Mining Bureau, I know that China understands that silver will be vital for their development and is currently looking to increase silver mining activity.

The Silver Institute had this to say recently: "In an effort to cultivate China's burgeoning silver industry, private investors are planning to build the Shanghai Silver Industry Exploitation Zone." Led by the Shanghai Contor Enterprise Development Company, the 500-acre zone will "enhance the competitiveness and status of the Chinese silver industry in the international market," officials said.

The development will be divided into several areas which include: production and processing of silver products, trade, logistics, business affairs, exhibition, information, scientific research, education and other services, and other relevant industries such as silver processing machinery, sensitive materials and electronics. The production and processing area will include deep processing, producing sensitization materials for electronics such as thick films, and an area devoted to silver antiseptic products.

The trade area will encompass a technical information and research exchange, an education area, a media area to publish books and papers about silver, a silver culture museum and garden, and a management area which will have a hotel, offices and restaurant.

Currently, China ranks fifth in the world in terms of silver production behind Mexico, Peru, Australia and the United States. China consumes 1,664 tons of silver annually, compared to 6,587 tons in the United States. With the opening of China's silver market, production and consumption are expected to rise significantly.

Shanghai was chosen as a silver center because of its strength as a center of business and finance. The development will be supported by an existing infrastructure including telecommunications, roads, communications, gas and electricity. The first phase of the project is scheduled to begin in 2005, with completion of the entire project by 2008.

The industrial demand due to China's rapid growth will only add to the pressures that industry already exerts on dwindling silver supplies. The use of silver in the electrical gird, the demand for TVs, computers, cell phones, batteries and other electronic devices will continue to grow in both India and China. This does not account for any investment demand from the Chinese populace. The Chinese have already embraced gold investing.

Another positive factor for silver is that China will be hosting the 2008 Olympics, and silver coin sets are produced for all modern Olympic events. Although perhaps a small factor, if the silver coin sets became popular among the Chinese people, with a population of 1.4 billion people, this could have a greater effect on the silver market than most realize.

Mexico is considering using its silver as a financial store of value. Some economists in Mexico have argued that the Mexican people have imported about as much U. S. paper as could ever be needed and it might be wise to recycle this paper back into the U.S.

The Mexican people are in favor of restoring silver in a monetary role presently. The Central Bank opposes this measure, but the jury is still out and there are politicians from all of Mexico's major parties that favor silver being used along side of the peso. Mr. Hugo Salinas Price has been instrumental in brining the idea of sound money to the population of Mexico and other Latin based countries.

This is not to be taken lightly because the Latin based countries are some of the largest silver producers in the world.

An interesting question to ask is "When or under what circumstances would silver (or gold) be the most valuable? This question poses some interesting aspects because it tests your own belief in the system. Do you trust the government or the source? The most important time may be when man made asset class loses value and is shunned in favor of something real. Since there are too many paper claims outstanding versus the amount of silver or gold available not everyone will be able to shift into a financial asset that has stood the test of five millennia.

Sooner or later, nearly everyone everywhere will catch on to the fact that the currency game is drawing to a close, that all fiat currencies are doomed. Action in the marketplace suggests this recognition is spreading; using gold backed Internet currencies, and the potential for a major silver producer (Mexico) to encourage its people to adopt a value based money system. A flight from all national currencies into real assets is gaining momentum and will accelerate. Ultimately people not government determine what money is and what money is not.

And, don't forget: the tremendous potential silver has as a component for technological advancement represents only half the story. The farther we move down the fiat money road, the greater the likelihood that we may ultimately see the investment demand for silver greatly exceed the industrial demand.

Thus, in spite of what you may hear in media reports about silver not being a good investment, or look to gold instead, I firmly believe that silver outlook remains decidedly positive.

Chapter 8

Silver bullion and coins

It has been a consistent view that the best silver investment anyone can make is in physical silver itself. There are a variety of reasons for this which we will examine in this chapter.

First, it should be pointed out that this writer was published in "The Investing Rules Book" and wrote the Ten Rules for Silver Investing. Rule number one follows;

Rule #1 - When all else fails, there is silver.

No one likes to be a prophet of doom, but the simple truth is that silver is the world's money of last resort. Should a severe economic collapse occur, leaving paper assets worthless, silver will be primary currency for purchase of goods and services. (Gold will be a store of major wealth, but will be priced too high for day-to-day use.) Thus, every investor should own some physical silver-and store a portion of it where it's accessible in an emergency.

Most people are familiar with investing in the stock market. Many are familiar with real estate investing, but very few know much about how to invest in precious metals. It is almost like stamp collecting to the general public, an interesting hobby that has very few participants.

This of course is only true over the past generation. Silver has actually been used in more places for longer periods of time as money than gold. Silver was the actual money used in the United States until 1965. Although gold is known as a monetary metal, it is used primarily for large transactions and for international settlements. When the U.S. went off the international gold standard in August 1971, gold was only used for international trade settlements. It was illegal for Americans to own gold at that time. However, Americans were able to own silver up until 1964. And then in 1965, President Johnson put us on what I call the "Johnson Slugs."

Which metal lasted longer in a monetary function for the people? For all practical purposes, gold ceased as a monetary function under Roosevelt in 1933, but silver pressed on until 1964. So just in fairly recent history you can observe silver's use as money was valid for thirty years longer than gold.

In any event, silver continued to act as money for the public at large. Silver was used as a merchant's metal. People were looking each other in the eyes to buy their food or lumber or to make a room addition on their homes; they used silver. I have nothing against gold. I am a gold bull and have been for a very long time and will continue to be. I just think silver doesn't get a fair shake. It isn't very well understood because very few people study it or know much about its monetary history.

Silver is certainly a much, much smaller market than gold. And gold is a tiny market compared to all kinds of other paper markets like the equity and treasury and bond markets.

It is interesting to look at silver as a money metal in today's world to give some perspective to how a paper monetary system can really distort values over time.

If we go back to using what many people refer to as "honest money" as a hypothetical exercise in may astound the reader. For sake of argument let us agree there is one billion ounces of silver in both bullion and coin form in the world today.

Now let us take that one billion ounces of silver and divide it among the 300 million people in the United States. That would be about three troy ounces of silver for everyone. In today's dollars it would be about $30 or so.

This gives a bit of a perspective as to how little money would be required to purchase the entire silver market. It also provides some perspective as to value.

When silver has been used as a monetary medium in the past it was generally accepted that a dollar per day was a medium wage. This was not a subsistence wage, but a working wage that was able to provide for a working family. A silver dollar is just over 3/4 of an ounce of silver but for illustration purposes we will use one ounce.

Today the minimum wage varies but can be in the vicinity of seven dollars per hour. So an eight hour day is worth just about $56.00. Therefore it could be suggested for your consideration that silver might be worth at least $50 in present value if not a great deal more.

The problem with silver at this time is lack of investment demand. Most people simply do not know how to invest in the metal. What is so amazing is that investing in precious metals is very easy. Almost anyone in any good size town or city can simply look up coins in the yellow pages of the phone book and find precious metals available.

However, the world is changing rapidly and anyone familiar with the internet can and will find many places where one can purchase either silver or gold. The problem is and always has been that people are reluctant to make a purchase where their check is cashed and they are dependent upon the honestly of the dealer to deliver the metal.

There is really very little to worry about, most dealers are honest and do deliver as promised, however every now and again a problem does occur. It is always best to start with a well recognized firm that has been in business for several years, and make your initial purchase a small one. That way if anything does goes wrong you have not made a large commitment.

Besides buying metal outright purchases can also be made through some internet sites that specialize in holding precious metals for their clients. Many of these have become available over the past few years, as the Internet has changed the way people conduct business in a very significant way.

One that we know and trust is located at www.goldmoney.com and was founded by James Turk whom we know personally. A client can purchase both gold and silver and have the metal stored for a very reasonable fee.

We do not sell coins or bullion, but have researched many dealers and have a special report available on our website, bullion sellers report. This report provides our exact transactions for several different precious metals dealers in the U.S. We have not researched a sound dealer network outside of the U.S. at this time.

Many times we are asked what is the best form of silver to purchase. Our answer has been to consistently begin with old silver coins, known as "junk silver" in the trade. Although, we do not see a time where you would have to rely upon silver coinage for daily expenses it has proven useful in the past.

Once the investor has established a core holding in silver coinage, then they can consider silver bars or bullion. In almost all cases 100 troy ounce bars or smaller versions (10oz for example) are good investor choices. The area that most investors should stay away from is a Comex grade bar of approximately 1000 troy ounces. Unless you are a very wealthy investor or a financial institution one thousand ounce bars are really not necessary. These bars are primarily used in industry and certainly are available to investors but pose special features that most investors do not want to deal with. For example transportation and assay requirements.

One thing new or even experienced investor should be aware of is the fact that many coin dealers will do their best to convince clients that they really need to purchase rare coins to avoid any potential confiscation issues. According to Franklin Sanders of www.themoneychanger.com "The sales pitches for their alleged safety rest on shaky assumptions about human nature and ignorance of the law. "Numismatic" coins were not exempted from the 1933 gold seizure, only "gold coins having a recognized special value to collectors of rare and unusual coins." [Exec. Ord. of 4/5/1933, ß 2(b)]." As Franklin correctly points out this law is vague and there is nothing at law today that makes rare coins any more or less secure than bullion coins. Numismatic dealers argue that because government exempted "numismatics" then, they must exempt them now, but that is faulty logic.

Another interesting fact, which receives little if any print is that U.S. citizens, can help to secure their future by having gold and or silver in their IRA accounts. The rules are a bit strict because the IRA must purchase coins minted by the U.S. Mint meaning gold or silver coins stamped by the U.S. Mint. It would make little sense that these bullion coins that are held by Americans for their individual retirement savings would be subject to confiscation. Again as Franklin Sanders points our, "by statute, the only coins defined as "numismatic" are American Eagle gold and silver coins minted since 1985 and other currently minted commemorative coins. No statute or regulation defines U.S. $20 gold pieces (or any other U.S. gold or silver coin) minted before 1935 as numismatic."

In most cases the markup on a rare coin is thirty percent and the markup on a bullion coin varies but can be as low as perhaps 3 percent for gold and around seven percent for silver in most cases. Obviously, the dealers much rather make a sale with a much higher markup.

This is not to blast the rare coin industry because in fairness rare coins can provide unbelievable price appreciation. Some rare coins have made their owners rich indeed. It is really outside the scope of this book to examine this area because it is highly specialized and if the reader is interested in this subset of the gold and silver markets it is suggested that one do a great deal of study and find a very reputable dealer that really knows the rare coin market.

Will silver coinage ever be needed as final payment in today's world? This is highly doubtful, most means of payment are electronic and we doubt a time will come where physical metal is widely accepted. However, there are some interesting considerations to be made regarding both gold and silver coins.

Passing through Los Angeles during the mid 1970's when the first Oil Embargo took place, we saw two private gas station owners set up pumps that would only accept payment in silver coinage. We point this out simply to let our readers know that the Free Market can provide some very interesting solutions in difficult times.

Another interesting thought regarding gold and silver is the ability to truly save in a form that is not dependent upon the health of the general financial markets. Our thought, get real, buy real, meaning that real gold and silver coins are a store of value and have been for thousands of years.

The precious metals themselves are the only asset class that moves inversely to all other asset classes. This means that if the stock market moves down, gold and silver usually move up. This is not necessarily true of gold mining stocks, in a large sell-off mining stocks are normally treated for what they are—STOCKS!!

Certainly mining stocks do offer some interesting potential but it must be known that only the real metal has the power of protection that no other investment has.

Finally, it must be remembered that the one financial fact that history bears out is this: all paper currencies eventually fail. The United States had the Continental during its very early beginning and with this in mind, the Founding Fathers' recent experience helped them determine the monetary basis set forth in the U.S. Constitution.

Chapter 9

Silver Stocks - How to Pick A Good Mining Company

One of the most frequent questions asked by investors is, "Where can I invest in precious metals to maximize returns?"

One way to obtain leverage in gold and silver is to purchase their respective mining shares. Before we begin this discussion the reader must bear several important points in mind.

First, a mining company no matter how big or strong is still a company with the same potential challenges of any type of business. In fact the mining business is one of the toughest in existence.

So, a mining share is a stock investment, not a gold or silver investment under strict definition. Any mining share is a derivative of gold or silver or some other tangible asset, but is NOT the asset itself.

Generally, mining shares respond to the price of gold and silver in a leveraged fashion.

Developing a mine usually requires an abundance of time and money. It can take five years or longer from the time a prospective property is identified until full production is achieved. Mills for the largest mines can cost an incredible amount of money. Think about it. Before mining can take place, the ore body needs to be defined through a drilling program. Based on results, a feasibility study needs to be completed. Recently, this phase has taken on significant demands based upon current environmental concerns. At every step so far there is considerable risk.

Exploration Risk

Not all exploration projects will lead to discovery. Many won't have enough of anything interesting that would generate share price gains.

Assay Risk

Some companies just release the 'good' assays. Salting a mine does occur. We only have to look at the Bre-X fiasco to know that drill results do not always "pan out." This is only part of the story though. For example, suppose you own a rich property, but do not have the financial capability to build a mine. You decide to sell your property. Now the prospective buyer will usually do some independent drilling and analysis and may reach a different valuation.

Management Risk

Who's got a long-term track record of success? Who doesn't? What is their track record? What is the exit strategy for shareholders? Does the management believe in Hedging? Leasing?

Financial Risk

Is the investment sound? How does it measure up against its peers? Is the bookkeeping accurate?

Trading Risk

How liquid is your investment? Is there Institutional involvement? How many shares trade? How big is the spread between bid and ask?

With many risks come potential rewards. Mining shares are leveraged to the price of the underlying asset gold or silver or both for example. The higher the cost of mining, the greater the ups and downs of profits and thus share price potentially. Profit volatility can be illustrated. Consider the increase in earnings for two different gold mines.

Mine X has a mining cost of $200 per ounce and Mine Y has a mining cost of $250 per ounce. Now let us consider the increase in earnings if gold rises from $300 to $325 per ounce.

Company	Profit at $300	Profit at $325	Change
Mine X	$100	$125	+25%
Mine Y	$50	$75	+50%
Gold			+8.3%

This example illustrates how a moderate increase in the price of gold can produce leverage of varying degrees for different mining companies. In this example, the higher cost producer shows increased leverage over the lower cost producer. This of course is only half the story. What happens if the price of gold drops from $300 to $275?

Company	Profit at $300	Profit at $275	Change
Mine X	$100	$75	-25%
Mine Y	$50	$25	-50%
Gold			-8.3%

89

High cost mines mean high leverage plus high risk. There are other considerations. For example, how do you determine political risk? What about geographical risk? The topography and climatic conditions may determine when mining activity can take place and when it is impossible. Another factor in geographic risk is how many properties does a company own? If the company holds only one property, then the risk is greater than another company that holds several properties in different countries. My point is that determining the best investment areas for mining companies involves as much art as it does science.

Quality + Safety = Maximum Returns

It is important to follow trends. If history is any guide, quality plus safety means maximum results. The bigger, low debt, low hedged or lightly hedged companies have been favored over all others. This has proven to be a solid methodology. It does not mean that information on possible high flyers should be avoided all together. But when smaller and less established companies are considered, it is the reader that is required to use discretion.

Investors are tempted to apply standard investment analysis to mining companies. This does not work well. Right now a majority of mining companies do not allow for a price to earnings analysis to be performed. This type of analysis is more useful in trying to determine a market peak. Very few mining securities offer an income stream. There are some that do. But there are others who have tried and failed. Sunshine Mining Corporation had a silver-backed bond at one time.

During the last precious metals bull market the Sunshine silver backed bond was considered to be one of the safest "silver investments" possible by Jerome Smith an author that focused much of his work on the silver market. Looking back of course we now know this was not the case.

So again, caution is the watchword because all stocks are risky, the very nature of stock investing makes it impossible to win on every single company that you chose to invest.

If it is not grown, it has to be mined.

The mining business is tough, very tough. Yet mining is important, vitally important. The Northwest Mining Association states, "If it is not grown, it has to be mined." Think about that for a minute. The entire financial complex is shifting from paper assets to tangible assets at this time, and these types of shifts take a long period of time, normally ten years or so.

It is not difficult to see that raw commodities always have value: food (agricultural commodities), clothing (cotton), transportation (oil), heating (natural gas), shelter (lumber).

Stock prices are based on many factors and influences. A good method is to look at how much silver or gold am I buying per dollar invested. The math involved to find this answer is not really all that complicated. However, understanding what this "rough cut" really means is complex because it is never an apple-to-apple comparison. Just because an investor has determined that company X has more ounces per dollar, does not make it a better buy. Some ore is easier to extract, some is easier to refine, other areas are easy to clean up and restore and others are not. The most important fact is whether the mine is an open pit or underground mine.

Diversification Still Tried and True

It is important to diversify in the metal area for several reasons. Any investor knows diversification is important and it applies to mining stocks as well. However, having lived through the first secular bull market in the metals, much of what I have written can be discounted by what I am about to write. The best market students study human nature because that is key to understanding how and why markets move.

A personal experience may illustrate better. The year was 1979 and many of the mining companies that I followed were exploding in price. I had a friend that was "late to the party" so to speak, but could not help but get caught up in the excitement. He had asked my opinion of various mining companies and I gave him some of my thoughts. I received a phone call from him about a month later it was now 1980. He sounded very excited, yet a little relieved. I asked Phil what was going on?

"Well, you know what you said about choosing a mining company?"

"Yes," I answered.

"It just did not sound right to me, I looked at what you said, but so many of those companies had moved up so much. I finally found one of the American exchanges and it was still around two bucks per share. It was named gold something. I bought it and four days later sold it for four dollars per share."

"Great," I exclaimed. "Sorry, but I never heard of that company."

Phil replied, "That is the craziest thing. They weren't a mining company at all. They just had gold in their name. Guess I sold it to someone else that thought it was a mining company too."

So the story goes. Phil was lucky. The point is that in a bull market people can get swept away with emotion. Phil's research was based upon a cheap stock that had gold in the name. We have experienced a similar situation with the dot com stock issues. Fear and greed motivate people. In fact, they can motivate normally sane people to do something that they might not ordinarily consider.

As an investor, it is most important to maximize your return while attempting to minimize risk as mush as practical. There are several mining companies that offer ample opportunities for speculation. This is the case now. Near the end of the coming mining boom, there will be several times as many companies. This will be an indication that the investment cycle has run it's course, but I do not expect to witness this for many more years.

A word about cheap stocks

It has been my experience that most penny stocks in the mining industry are far too risky for the average investor. The problem is that many "investors" read speculators in this area love cheap stocks. The odds are stacked against you as an investor. For every 2000 mining claims only one actually becomes a mine. Most of these companies raise money, and promote and drill at the same time. The drill results for an exploration company are what usually move the stocks price up or down.

Human nature seems to love the idea that by investing in the right company one can become rich. This does happen but it is rare. However, people seem to zero in on this rare event and think, me too, my little junior exploration company is the next big winner.

Certainly there are a few exceptions in the industry that have better probability of success than others. In some cases an unknown company holds a well-defined asset, or perhaps a major mining concern has signed over a well-defined project to a smaller company because it is leaving the region.

A good rule of thumb for any junior mining company is to simply adhere to strict discipline and speculate with money you can afford to lose. As the precious metals sector continues to gather more interest more money will flow into the mining shares and the cheap stocks will get a lift.

If history repeats itself and the precious metals market repeats itself by ending in a mania, similar to the internet bubble, almost any company with gold or silver in the name will shoot up temporally. As a very astute observer once said "When the wind is strong enough, even the turkeys will fly."

A final note on investing in precious metals:

Mining equities can be fun and exciting especially when you have a stock that is appreciating in price. It must be known that nothing can be more disheartening than being correct about a sector, for example the precious metals sector and seeing your precious metals stock not keep up with the overall sector.

This can and does happen, and therefore empirical evidence demands that you spread out or diversify in this sector. The investor should also do his or her own due diligence and it is highly recommended to use an investment professional.

There is some help available through various sources such as independent newsletter writers than can offer opinions on various aspects of the markets. These have been useful but these should be used in our view as a tool or starting point for the investor.

It is well understood that the most important investment to be made in either silver or gold is in the actual metal itself. This point has been made several times, but it bears repeating. There have been many times in the monetary history of the world when only the real metal is of any practical value. For example, when the "boat people" were leaving Vietnam, gold coins could buy passage – but those who tried signing the back of their stock certificates as a means of payment are still waiting for the boat. Most investors know that, in order to build a well-structured metals portfolio, you need a hierarchy. First, real metal, bought and paid for; secondly, the shares of top-tier mining companies; and, lastly, investments with extreme leverage, but only for those with adequate risk capital.

Chapter 10

Other Leveraged silver investments

As if mining stocks did not provide enough leverage there are still other avenues that offer even more leverage than mining shares. The decision to use leverage in a precious metals purchase is a decision to accept a greater percentage of risk relative to your capital outlay.

The potential is for an increased opportunity to earn a greater percentage of profit. The use of leverage should match your risk tolerance, both from a financial and psychological point of view. The increased risk in using leverage is not worth it for most people.

It is my opinion that more damage has been done to the precious metals markets and in particular silver by the use of leverage than any other factor. This statement cannot be proven and again is opinion, however let us look at a typical scenario that has been repeated thousand upon thousands of times over the past quarter century.

A novice will do some preliminary research or reading and discover that silver has a supply demand relationship that is very favorable. Using this "knowledge" silver seems like a "no brainier" and this eager novice decides to use all the leverage available.

This fledgling investor opens a futures account, puts in the minimum margin required by the broker, goes "long" or buys silver on margin and within a very short time is wiped out. At that point this novice does not take personal responsibility for the loss, but instead blames someone or something else.

The first area might be the data or supply fundamentals must be incorrect or reported falsely. The tragedy is that this potential silver investor usually gets a bad taste for silver and will not ever enter the silver market again, but also joins the bearish camp in many instances.

Some of these people frequent Internet chat rooms and extol their "knowledge" about why silver is a poor performer.

First paper silver does not equal real silver. That is all silver derivates whether stocks, options, futures, leverage purchases, pool accounts, or exchange traded funds—all are derived from the asset silver but the real silver backing the transaction is not available for settlement. This is an important point, you may buy into some type of investment that is silver "backed" but by contract all you can receive is paper settlement, in other words a check.

This is total conjecture on our part but is used to illustrate an important point. Most futures accounts require a minimum of $5000 or so to open. Over the past few years the precious metals have been in a bull market, but both gold and silver experience long bear markets of over twenty years.

Let us suppose that during the twenty year bear market in silver where $5000 would have bought approximately one thousand ounces of silver. It is impossible to know how many futures accounts are opened and closed in any one-year period but a conservative look at silver trading shows the non-reportable positions to be in the order of 50,000 contracts. The non-reportable category is the little guy, the small "player" however look at perhaps half of the amount for this illustration.

Let us use 25,000 contracts on an annual basis for silver, which would represent 125 million ounces of silver (25,000 contracts x 5000 ounces per contract). This is a rather startling number considering that the entire Comex silver supply is about 125,000 as of early 2006.

Consider all of the silver futures traders that have lost money over the past 20 years and you start to comprehend how different the silver market price dynamics might have been if silver were a cash market only. This means no futures trading, but simply a cash and carry activity where investors and fabricators alike would buy silver at the current market price, which would vary due to the physical supply and the actual demand.

Before the reader asserts that a futures market must exist in all commodities, let us suggest for your consideration that eggs, potatoes, and milk used to have futures markets but no longer. All of those commodities still exist and the price setting mechanism is still intact.

Sources of Leverage

Futures

Futures brokers are licensed brokers with the Commodity Futures Trading Commission, who deal on exchanges such as the New York Commodity Exchange, Chicago Board of Trade and other areas. Acting as agents, using an open outcry system, the price for a given commodity is established. Purchasing silver from a futures broker requires that the individual put up a good-faith deposit. This deposit assures the broker that the investor will meet the contractual requirements.

Leveraged dealers

Leveraged dealers are authorized to offer investors the ability to buy and sell precious metals on a margined basis. The agreement between a leveraged dealer and his/her customer is a legal contract. Transactions are conducted on the basis of this contract.

Leveraged dealers are the principals in all transactions and establish the bid and ask prices on a variety of precious metals investments. Leverage dealers maintain the ability to meet their obligations to customers with physical inventories, futures contracts, and at times swaps and forward positions.

A leveraged contract allows the purchaser to take delivery upon full payment of the balance due. This is very close to a futures contract. The leveraged contract evolved during the late 1960s in response to the growth of investor interest in United States of America silver coins. Coin dealers began to sell bags of U.S. coins to the public on a cash basis. Since the maximum a purchaser could lose was the difference between the face value of the coins and the value of the silver content of the coins. Customers began to finance coin purchases pledging the coins as security for the loan. This method of leverage became very popular during the previous bull market in precious metals.

Leverage has a price

The bottom line is when you purchase precious metals with leverage you are using credit. All forms of credit subject you to interest charges, in a futures contract the out going months are priced higher based upon the current cash price plus the going short-term interest rate. This cost is referred to as the "contango" or the "Carrying charge." Each month into the future becomes more expensive on an incremental basis.

Generally, futures trading is done on a lower commission charge than banks or leveraged dealers. There are exceptions to this general rule however. In an inflationary environment the monetary unit in question loses value, this permits a borrower to pay down the loan with less valuable units of exchange. So, in an inflationary condition borrowing to purchase precious metals seems to make sense.

However, because the price movement is amplified to the investor both up and down many investors have learned the hard way that leverage in not always a smart decision. Unfortunately, most folks use too much leverage, do not have a plan in place if the market moves against their original purchase order, and do not have sufficient capital to be in a leveraged condition to begin with.

If the metals market moves to such an extent that the investor no longer has sufficient equity then the purchaser (borrower) is subject to a "call" for additional funds. If a margin call is made, the investor is required to send funds within a very short time frame. If funds are not received within the period specified, all or a portion of the account is liquidated to satisfy the investor's contractual obligations. This can be a very discouraging situation and would not happen had the investor chosen either to make a cash purchase, or used a suitable amount of leverage relative to the investor's capitalization.

Whether one should meet a margin call or liquidate a position is a personal choice. Many differing attitudes exist, ranging from never meeting a margin call (cut your loss) to making additional purchases (averaging on the way down). Whatever the individual choice you must be prepared to take the appropriate action.

It is best to bear in mind that most who enter into futures end up losing money. The professionals are very good in their abilities to trade the markets and most individuals are not. Being free market oriented it is certainly a personal choice whether you chose to use leverage and we support your decision, but be prepared all markets go up and down and you could be correct about the overall trend and still lose money on a short term move against the primary trend.

Chapter ⑪

The Future of Silver

The future of silver is bright indeed. The most important factor that has kept silver from really exploding until recently is so little investor interest. Gold has enjoyed a great deal of investor interest the past several months and certainly some of this has spilled over into the silver market.

The main reason that investor interest has accelerated recently is that the SEC has approved a silver Exchange Traded Fund. This investment product will allow investors of all levels professional and private investor alike to participate in the silver market. The main concerns for most potential silver investors is how to buy silver, and once purchased, where is silver stored. The Silver ETF eliminates these two concerns.

Since silver has demonstrated its ability to move up quickly and strongly and also correct in a rather harsh manner, we wanted to give a longer term perspective on price analysis for our readers. Of course no one can guarantee that any investment will reach a certain price, so with that said, it might be best to follow the logic. First we look at the theoretical price of gold and once that is established then we look at what that might mean for the silver price.

If we look at the reported M1(Money Supply) figures from the Federal Reserve we can determine the theoretical price of gold for any period. For example most often quoted is the fact that gold soared to

$800 per ounce in early 1980. If we take the currency component in 1980 of 105.144 Billion dollars and divide it by 262 Million ounces (the reported US gold holdings) We find the dollar price of gold to be $400.00. That is $105M/262M = $400, using figures in the public domain for 1980. We know for a fact that gold sold briefly for over double that amount, over $800 per ounce in January 1980.

Now if we fast-forward to our condition at the beginning of the new millennium, we find that the M1 supply in early 2000 was reported to be 523.078 Billion. Doing the math again yields a quotient of over $2000 per ounce.

Does this mean the price of gold is going to reach $2000 per ounce? Possibly, but if we stick with known facts, we find something very interesting. Now in 2006 the number is more like $2500 per ounce. Many in the industry are suggesting $3000 to $5000 dollar per ounce gold.

First, as any gold bug will tell you, regardless of what the mainstream financial press reports, the money supply has increased dramatically in the past 30 years and continues to do so because the Federal Reserve has committed to inflate their way out of any problems.

Secondly, the Treasury held gold has remained constant. Lastly, gold has the potential to overshoot the currency price. A troy ounce of gold has the same mass anywhere in the entire universe. That is an unchanging objective truth that no one, not gold bears, bullion bankers, stockbrokers, the CFTC or the World Gold Council, can change. However, a "dollar" (read Federal reserve note) has an upper limit that is not a strictly held value. The money supply or amount of dollars has no upper limit. Perhaps if all "dollars" were actual currency it might be restricted by the number of trees on earth but since the currency supply is a mere 5% of the total money supply, the vast majority being held in computer memory the point is mute.

The salient point is that the number on a piece of paper (or amount of zero's added to computer memory) can literally be moved so close to infinity that for all practical purposes it is infinite. Before you argue that this is a rather subjective argument I would ask the reader to verify with the Federal Reserve itself just exactly what percentage of a 1913-dollar the current "dollar" is worth. You would verify that 96% of the value is gone and a current "note" is worth about 4 cents of what a 1913-dollar was. Although this allows the fact that a FRN ("dollar") is worth something most of its value has slipped away.

So if we go back to our basic function, the price of gold. We must look at paper money over time, and we have determined that unbacked paper money over time always loses value. In fact the value of paper money approaches zero over time. We already know that the "dollar" has lost 96% of its value as stated by the Federal Reserve Board, the very body whose stated purpose is to keep the value of the money stable. (Fine job gentlemen!) So the basic function or equation we are working with is simple, to determine

the paper price of gold or perhaps better stated the dollar price of gold, we need to take something that is so plentiful that it's value approaches zero (paper money supply), divided by something of real value, (gold).

This might be expressed as $/oz. or "dollars" per ounce. This of course is exactly what we did earlier in this article. However, we are now advanced math students and we will also use our thinking to put into the equation what happens to the numerator over time. Weknow for an absolute fact that the numerator (money supply) grows ever larger; in fact in time it approaches infinity.

So now the equation can be expressed as infinity divided by a real number. For those not familiar with the rules of advanced math do not take my word for it but the idea is the $/oz or infinite ability to expand the money supply divided by a finite amount of gold equals infinity!! Yes, that is correct the paper price of gold over time approaches infinity. This of course is in theory, but illustrates an important point.

How readers can we use this to help us?

First I would ask that you truly ponder this. Does it make sense? Is the money supply created out of thin air? Who determines how many dollars are in existence at any given period of time? Next, I would ask the reader to again take a look back to see if we can find any facts that support this hypothesis. I will provide one; your job is to prove to yourself that a currency crisis won't happen again and WHY?

The rentenmark is an example of the limit of paper money. The world witnessed this event in Germany following W.W.I. Just prior to the currency crisis, politicians and government economists made loud claims the economy was prospering.

Our greatest concern is not the facts stated above but the theory that the next precious metals run will be one generated by FEAR of a currency collapse. Yes, friends there was fear in the late 1970's but most people were buying gold based on the increase in money supply and inflation figures.

Today, the Money supply is scarcely mentioned in the press and the reported inflation numbers leave out such non-essentials as food and oil. What would cause the kind of FEAR that we see? What would cause a major run to gold by any of the United States trading partners? Why did Nixon close the international gold window? When France sent enough American paper in exchange for that barbarous relic GOLD.

Once a country or even a major bank decides to save it's own currency and starts to exchange bonds for gold the game will be over. Will this happen? Actually it is happening at this time, Cheuvreux, the equity brokerage house of Credit Agricole, the huge French bank, in early February 2006 distributed a 56-page report that completely endorses in detail the findings of the Gold Anti-Trust Action Committee that the price of gold has been surreptitiously suppressed by Western central banks and that those banks do not have the gold they claim to have.

Now getting to silver. Keep in mind that there is less available. From recent history, we know that silver, because it is a smaller market, tends to move faster. We could look at the average ratio of silver to gold. Let's say we have silver at a 50-to-1 ratio would give us a $50 dollar silver price (it's old high). However, if silver accelerated and got back to it's classic ratio of 16-to-1, that would put silver at over $150 per ounce. Lastly, if silver ever went to it's natural ratio that is the ratio at which it is found in the earth of 10-to-1, then $250 ounce silver is possible. I know this sounds absurd, but chance favors the prepared mind. If you are not willing to accept my basic premise, then ignore the rest.

These price projections may seem much too optimistic and perhaps time will prove them to be overstated. But in light of fairly recent history it would be beneficial to the reader to study a monthly chart of palladium over the past ten years. The palladium monthly chart would be a fair representation of price expectations for silver. Palladium came off a long base and a very tight price pattern. One the price started to rise more and more investors and speculators entered the market. The market exhibited some extreme volatility but on a price spike palladium went over $1100.00 USD. Had anyone bought the metal when it was totally out of favor and held on, the potential is obvious from price history.

Silver could easily exhibit similar characteristics, but it is a metal that is more familiar than palladium, can be purchased much more easily and has a solid track record as being a valuable asset during times of inflation.

What about something nobody is looking at right now, which is a monetary crisis? Many countries have had massive currency problems and their citizens had dramatic problems. In the U.S., you have record trade deficits, balance of trade problems, and the Euro, which is strong competition to the U.S. dollar. What would happen to the price of silver, if in a monetary crisis, you get investment demand for silver and gold?

You could not put a paper price on silver and gold in a true monetary panic. It would be very high because the markets for both metals are so small. The problem of a currency crisis is rather small however; the U.S. has basically had a "slow motion" currency crisis over the past several decades.

People adjust to what they are taught without really thinking for themselves or putting the ideas presented into the context of history. Today people are taught to think inflation is normal and some inflation is required for the economy to be strong, not knowing that history teaches that any currency severed from a value basis eventually causes severe economic problems.

As these problems manifest the establishment is usually ready with very important sounding explanations never admitting the true cause of the problem—trying to get something for nothing. In fact what has occurred in the past is the nasty speculators are sometimes blamed for causing the problem.

This of course is human nature the few that understand what is really happening take action to satisfy the inherent human need for security, while those in positions of power really do not understand the basic truths of sound financial systems –value for value.

Time to Take Action!!

Now that you have read this book you are probably wondering just how to invest in this exciting market and maximize your profits and keep your risk minimal. We have a solution for you and best of all it is FREE! You should go to our website www.silver-investor.com and immediately sign up for the Free Email Newsletter. You will receive the Ten Rules of Silver Investing over the next ten days.

Since Mr. Morgan's experience in the precious metals spans 30 years his monthly publication "The Morgan Report" gives specific investment opinions on mining companies both producers and speculative exploration type of companies. The report is not advertised as a timing tool, but Mr. Morgan has put out some very good calls intermediate tops and bottoms. This is a paid report and is separate from the Free email letter. Our subtitle on the website is "The Official Site for the Serious Metals Investor." Bottom line if you want expert opinion to help guide you through we think a mere $60.00 USD for a six month trial subscription is well within the ability of any serious investor. We cannot guarantee this low price much longer but the full year subscription is only $99.00 USD and considered the best report on silver and resource investing in the business.

Many that are getting started ask a very important question about making gold and silver purchases and a special report is available on the website. See Silver Bullion Sellers on the website www.silver-investor.com. In almost all of our work subscribers receive a discount on any material we produce.

Mr. Morgan can been heard each week on the Internet at www.financialsense.com.

Mr. Morgan does speak at Investment Conferences around the world so be sure to check out the website for the most current information.

Many people think knowledge is power but they are incorrect, knowledge by itself is simply knowledge--Power comes from taking action, so take action today get on the free mailing list and start to build your education about money, the economy, finance, personal wealth building, and a host of other topics.

You are one mouse click away from becoming more powerful in your financial affairs.

To Contact us go to www.silver-investor.com and hit the contact button on the website.

LaVergne, TN USA
10 October 2010
200229LV00001B/48/P